# ANALOGICAL REASONING IN
# CHILDREN

# Analogical Reasoning in Children

## Usha Goswami
### *University of Cambridge*

LAWRENCE ERLBAUM ASSOCIATES, PUBLISHERS
Hove                                    Hillsdale (USA)

Lawrence Erlbaum Associates Ltd., Publishers
27 Palmeira Mansions
Church Road
Hove
East Sussex, BN3 2FA
U.K.


British Library Cataloguing in Publication Data

Goswami, Usha
Analogical Reasoning in Children.—
(Essays in Developmental Psychology Series, ISSN 0959-3977)
I. Title  II. Series
155.4

ISBN 0-86377-226-9 (Hbk)
ISBN 0-86377-324-9 (Pbk)


Printed and bound in the United Kingdom by BPCC Wheatons Ltd., Exeter

*To Peter and Ann*

# Contents

# Preface

This book took much longer to write than I expected. I began it in Oxford, supported by a Junior Research Fellowship from Merton College, and continued it during periods of leave from Cambridge, which were partly spent at the Department of Psychology, University of Illinois at Urbana-Champaign, supported by a Spencer Post-Doctoral Fellowship. To these institutions and funding bodies, I give my thanks. I would also like to thank a number of colleagues who have helped to shape my thinking as I wrote this book: Ann Brown, Judy Deloache, Keith Stanovich, Jerry De Jong, Brian Ross and Dedre Gentner in America; Tony Dickinson, Norman Freeman and Peter Bryant in England; and most especially Renée Baillargeon in Illinois and Josef Perner in Sussex, both of whom provided me with extremely detailed feedback on many chapters.

Usha Goswami
*Cambridge, May 1992*

# CHAPTER ONE

# Reasoning by Analogy

Reasoning by analogy is a central component of human cognition. It is involved in classification and in learning, it provides a tool for thought and explanation, and it is important for scientific discovery and creative thinking. Its fundamental role in reasoning has been widely recognised in cognitive psychology, where it has been the focus of recent research in areas as diverse as learning by example, the nature of conceptual structure, creative problem solving, and artificial intelligence (e.g. see Vosniadou & Ortony, 1989). The importance of analogical reasoning has also been widely documented in the history of science.

Many classic scientific discoveries were made by analogy. A famous example is that of Archimedes (3rd century B.C.), who had been asked to determine whether base metal had been substituted for gold in an intricately designed crown ordered by his king. Although the weight per volume of pure gold was known, the crown was so ornate that its volume was impossible to measure. Archimedes was unable to see a solution to this problem until he went home and stepped into the bath. He then saw an analogy between the volume of water displaced by his body as he got into his bath, and the volume of water that would be displaced by the crown. The problem was solved. By immersing the crown in water, he could work out whether it was made of pure gold.

Another famous example of analogy in science is Kepler's analogy between religion and the relationship between the motion of the planets and their distance from the sun. He wrote: "My ceaseless search

1

concerned primarily three problems, namely the number, size and motion of the planets ... by that beautiful analogy between the stationary objects, namely the sun, the fixed stars, and the space between them, with God the Father, the Son, and the Holy Ghost." The analogy mapped out as follows: "The sun in the middle of the moving stars, himself at rest and yet the source of motion, carries the image of God the Father and Creator. He distributes his motive force through a medium which contains moving bodies, even as the Father creates through the Holy Ghost" (cited in Gordon, 1979). This analogy eventually led Keppler to an operational theory of celestial mechanics that resulted in the notion of gravity.

Kepler's discovery also illustrates an important point about the role of analogy in the history of science, a point which applies equally to Aristotle. Most analogical breakthroughs were not miraculous in the sense that their discoverers took a step into the complete unknown. Instead, much of the conceptual preparation for the discoveries had already taken place, and it was probably only a matter of time before somebody made the analogical connection. Nevertheless, the discoverers did make a genuine contribution to the development of knowledge, as their analogies provided a genuinely new way of thinking about previously known phenomena. This point was put succinctly in 1909 by the French mathematician Poincaré, who noted the creative role played by analogies in theory development in mathematics: "the mathematical facts worthy of being studied are those which, by their analogy with other facts, are capable of leading us to the knowledge of a mathematical law just as experiential facts lead us to the knowledge of a physical law. They are those which reveal to us unsuspected kinship between other facts, long known, but wrongly believed to be strangers to one another" (cited in Gordon, 1979). The role of conceptual knowledge (the facts) in successful analogising will be one of the themes of this book.

Analogies are often used to teach science as well. A familiar example is using hydrostatics as an analogy for electricity, with the behaviour of flowing water providing an analogue for the activity of the electricity. The wire or conductor of the electricity is likened to a pipe through which the water flows, the battery is similar to a pool or reservoir, electrical voltage is analogous to water pressure, and a resistor is like a restriction in the water pipe. The fact that the presence of a resistor will decrease electrical current in a wire can then by understood by analogy to a restriction in a water pipe which will decrease the water flow in that pipe. Similarly, the fact that an increase in voltage occurs when two batteries are connected in series is explained by analogy to the increase in water pressure that would result from connecting two reservoirs of water that differed in height. However, prior conceptual knowledge will play a role here, too. Useful pedagogical analogies depend on a certain degree of knowledge on the part of the student: the relevant relationships within the conceptual system on which the analogy is based must already be understood. A student who did not understand hydrostatics would not learn anything about electricity from the preceding analogy.

Analogies can facilitate problem-solving as well as learning and discovery, as many experiments have shown. For example, Gick and Holyoak (1980, 1983) designed a paradigm based on Duncker's X-ray problem to investigate the benefits conferred by analogy. In Duncker's problem, surgeons need to destroy an internal tumour with X-rays without simultaneously destroying the surrounding healthy tissue. It is impossible to use invasive surgery, as the patient will die. The solution is to use a number of weak X-rays that individually will not harm body tissue, and to achieve the appropriate strength by converging the rays onto the tumour. Only 5% of Duncker's students thought of this "convergence solution" spontaneously.

Gick and Holyoak's idea was to tell their subjects about an appropriate analogy prior to presenting them with Duncker's problem. The analogy concerned a famous general who had successfully captured a fortress surrounded by mined approach roads. Although the general needed the strength of his entire army to capture the fortress, the weight of all his men was bound to trigger the mines. The general solved this problem by dividing his army into smaller units that were too light to set off the mines, and then sending each unit down a separate road, so that they converged onto the fortress in a united attack. Students who learned about this analogy were more likely to think of the "convergence solution" to Duncker's problem. So the right analogy can significantly improve problem-solving performance.

Analogies are thus important in learning, problem solving and discovery. Surprisingly, however, developmental psychology has been less ready to assign a central role to analogical reasoning. In fact, children's use of analogy was not widely studied until fairly recently. The reasons for this neglect were partly historical. According to Piagetian theory, the ability to reason by analogy was a late-developing skill, emerging at around 11–12 years of age during the "formal-operational" period of reasoning. Younger children were thought to be incapable of reasoning by analogy, and consequently few people investigated their analogical reasoning skills.

The traditional view of analogical development was supported by research in psychometrics. Psychometric research had shown that many children, even at 11–12 years of age, were unable to complete simple analogies like *pig:boar::dog:* ? (wolf). When given these analogies, younger children typically produced non-analogical associative responses, like *pig:boar::dog:cat* (e.g. Achenbach, 1971). Psychometricians used these "item" or "classical" analogies as a measure of I.Q., regarding them as a test of the development of reasoning skills. Let us begin by examining the kind of reasoning that these tests of analogy require in more detail.

## Classical Analogies

The term "classical analogy" is derived from Aristotle. He defined analogy as "an equality of proportions ... involving at least 4 terms ... when the second is related to the first as the fourth is to the third" (Aristotle, *Metaphysics*). Aristotle's definition of analogy concentrates on the need to equate the relations between the pairs of terms in the analogy, which are usually represented by the format A:B::C:D (e.g. *wide:narrow::high:low*). The relation between the C and the D terms should be equivalent to that linking the A and the B terms.

This "relational similarity" requirement is made very clear in most standardised tests of analogical reasoning, as the instructions from one such test demonstrate: "In each of the sequences below, Figure A is to Figure B as Figure C is to ONE of the Figures D. Choose the Figure in D that bears the same relation to Figure C as Figure B does to Figure A" (NFER Picture Test A, Stuart, 1977). An analogy item from this test is shown in Fig. 1.1. Younger children typically do more poorly than older children on these tests.

Aristotle's criterion of an equality of relations is generally accepted to be the "hallmark" of analogical reasoning. According to the traditional view, younger children are unable to reason by analogy because they are incapable of using this hallmark. They do not understand relational similarity. The tendency of younger children to solve analogies by producing associative responses provides apparent support for this view.

For example, Gallagher and Wright (1977) asked a group of 10-year-olds to complete verbal multiple-choice classical analogies like *food:body::rain:* (water, storm, coat, *ground*). Most children selected the incorrect response *water*, explaining their choice with justifications such as "Water falls from the sky". These justifications ignored relational similarity. Piaget and his colleagues gave 5- to 6-year-olds a classical analogy task based on pictures, and found a similar failure to equate relations. For example, Bol. (aged 6 years, 6 months) was given some pictures that included the analogy *nurse:syringe::barber:scissors*. He selected the pictures of the nurse and of the syringe, then took the picture of the barber and paused, non-plussed: "I'm looking for a washbasin" (Piaget, Montangero & Billeter, 1977).

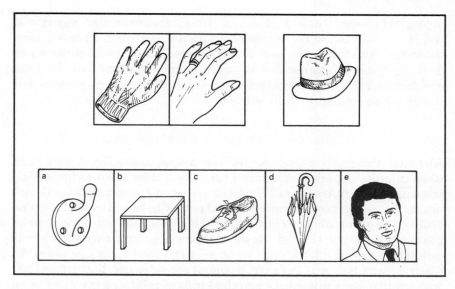

FIG. 1.1. A typical picture analogy from the NFER Picture Test A (reproduced with permission from Stuart, 1977.).

## Problem Analogies

A different approach to studying analogical reasoning in children is to give them problems to solve by analogy. Research using this approach initially seemed to support the idea that younger children could not use relational correspondences. In the "problem analogy" paradigm, the relational similarity that children have to reason about is between two problems and their solutions. The children are told about one problem, usually called the *base* problem, and are then given a similar problem to solve, usually called the *target* problem. The assumption is that children who can recognise and use relational similarity should solve the target problem by using an analogous solution to that in the base.

In one such experiment, young children (5–6 years) learned about a base problem in which a magic genie rolled his carpet into a tube to provide a passage for some precious jewels. This was meant to provide an analogy to the target problem, which involved transporting some small rubber balls from one location to another. The children were expected to work out that a possible solution to this problem was to roll up a sheet of paper that had been provided by the experimenters, and make a passage for the balls. The relational similarity was meant to be "rolling up a flat and flexible object" (Holyoak, Junn & Billman, 1984). However, the majority of children failed to see the intended relational correspondence between the carpet and the paper, and totally ignored the sheet of paper when devising their solutions. The relational similarity between the base problem and the target problem was evident to the experimenters, but it was not so evident to their subjects.

### "Higher-order" vs "Lower-order" Relations

Although the classical and the problem analogy paradigms have been used in quite separate research literatures, they seem to be testing the same basic reasoning skills. Both are trying to measure children's ability to recognise and to use similarities between relations. The ability to reason about relational similarity would not appear to be particularly sophisticated. However, the claim that this ability was not present until adolescence went unchallenged for many years. To discover why this was the case, we must consider the distinction that was traditionally made between the kinds of relations involved in an analogy.

There was a pervasive belief that two levels of reasoning were involved in analogy, and that these corresponded to the apprehension of two different kinds of relations. In classical analogies, the two kinds of relation were (1) lower-order or first-order relations, and (2) higher-order or second-order relations (e.g. Lunzer, 1965; Inhelder & Piaget, 1958). The distinction between these two kinds of relation was believed to have psychological reality.

"Lower-order" relations are traditionally defined as the relations between the A and the B terms and between the C and the D terms in an analogy. For example, in the analogy *bird:feathers::dog:hair*, the "lower-order" relations relate the different elements in each pair of terms, such as *birds* and *feathers*. One possible "lower-order" relation would be "enables flight", as the aerodynamic properties of feathers help birds to fly. Another possible "lower-order" relation would be "keeps warm", as feathers help to protect birds from the cold.

These "lower-order" relations are thought to be an ontologically simpler kind of relation than "higher-order" relations. "Higher-order" relations link the "lower-order" relations, so a "higher-order" relation is a relationship between the pairs of elements in the analogy. The "higher-order" relation in the analogy *bird:feathers::dog:hair* would be something like "protective covering". "Higher-order" relations are believed to require a more complex kind of reasoning than "lower-order" relations, as they are "second-order" relations. The two kinds of relation are shown in Fig. 1.2.

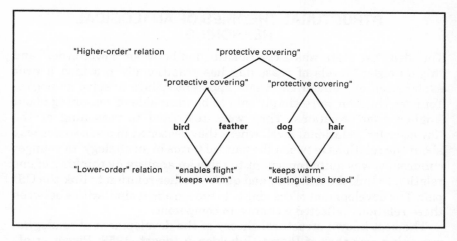

FIG. 1.2. The traditional view of the two sets of relations in an analogy.

A similar distinction between two levels of reasoning is found in problem analogies. The distinction here is usually between reasoning about the relations in a given problem, and reasoning about the objects in which those relations are embedded. Younger children and novice reasoners have been thought to focus on the objects at the expense of the relations between them (Gentner, 1983, 1989). For example, in the genie analogy mentioned earlier, younger children might focus on the genie and his carpet rather than on the "rolling" solution. This would lead them to look for similar *objects* in the rubber balls problem, and so they would ignore similar relations.

Older children and more expert reasoners are thought to focus on relational commonalities when trying to solve analogies, enabling them to extract "higher-order" structure. They go beyond the "mere appearance" of the objects in the base and the target problems, and reason about the relations between them. In the genie analogy, expert reasoners would focus on the "rolling a flexible material" relation, ignoring the superficial dissimilarity between the sheet of paper and the carpet. In richer problem analogies with many relations, expert reasoners would focus on "higher-order relations with inferential import" rather than on isolated relations (Gentner, 1983). For example, in Rutherford's analogy between a hydrogen atom and the solar system (both are orbiting systems), expert reasoners would focus on the cause–effect relations that govern orbiting rather than on isolated relations such as the sun being hotter than the planets.

## STRUCTURAL THEORIES OF ANALOGICAL REASONING

The idea that there was a clear distinction between "lower-order" and "higher-order" levels of reasoning has traditionally provided a neat explanation of younger children's apparent failure to solve analogies. Younger children were simply said to be incapable of reasoning about "higher-order" relations. They were restricted to reasoning at the "lower-order" relational level, where they reasoned in a *successive* way about the relations between the pairs of terms in an analogy. To younger children, it was quite consistent to solve an analogy by thinking of one relation to link the A:B pair, and quite another relation to link the C:D pair. The development of the ability to reason about similarities between these relations reflected a change in competence.

The best-known structural theory of the development of analogical reasoning was that of Piaget (Inhelder & Piaget, 1958; Piaget et al., 1977), who placed this change in analogical competence at around 11–12 years of age. Children younger than 11–12 years of age could not reason by analogy, and children older than 11–12 years of age could. Researchers in the Piagetian tradition succeeded in amassing a respectable body of evidence in support of this predicted shift in analogical ability, as we will see. They also showed that, prior to adolescence, children indeed seemed to reason successively about the relations in analogies.

Structural theories depend on three related assumptions, however, all of which are debatable. One is that it is possible to make a clear distinction between "higher-order" relations and "lower-order" relations. This assumption is critical, as according to structural theories younger children can only reason about the latter. The second assumption, which is very important for testing the theory, is that children younger than 11 years of age know the relations involved in the analogies that they are asked to solve. To test the theory properly, it is crucial that their problem is not one of lack of knowledge, but of constructing the "higher-order" relations. The third assumption is that the children understand the objective of the task, namely that the correct solution to an analogy involves relational *similarity* rather than just finding relationships between terms. Let us examine each of these assumptions more closely.

### 1. The Assumption of Hierarchical Relations

The first assumption made by structural theorists was quite simply wrong. In reality, it is impossible to decide *a priori* which relations in an analogy are "lower-order" and which are "higher-order". This classification is actually made *after* the solution to the analogy is known. For example, in the analogy *bird:feathers::dog:hair*, the traditional account would label the relation "protective covering" as the "higher-order" relation, as it applies to both pairs of terms in the analogy. In the analogy *food:body::rain:ground*, the "higher-order" relation would be "nurtures". Yet a subject presented with the first two terms in these analogies could easily designate these as "lower-order relations" (e.g. "Birds and feathers are related because feathers keep birds warm", or "Food and the body are related because food provides fuel for the body"). So it is not clear *a priori* whether these relations are "higher-order" relations or "lower-order" relations.

It follows that it is impossible to argue that *different* classical analogies involve *different* "higher-order" relations. In fact, the relation at the top of the hierarchy will always be the same: that of similarity or equivalence of the "lower-order" relations. This is the hallmark of analogy according to the classical account. The distinction between the relations that are "lower-order" and those that are "higher-order" is thus a matter of terminology. It may not have psychological reality. The decision about whether the "higher-order" relation in the analogy *bird:feathers::dog:hair* is "protective covering" or "similarity of the 'lower-order' relations" depends on representational choices made by the theorist. This alternative view of the relations in an analogy is shown in Fig. 1.3.

The same point about terminology applies to the relations in problem analogies. Here the "higher-order" relations can be specified

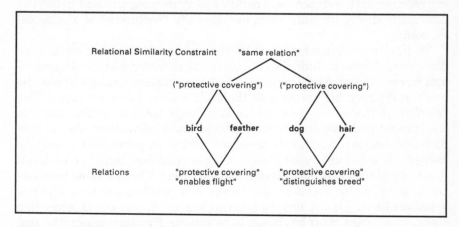

FIG. 1.3. An alternative view of the two sets of relations in an analogy.

syntactically by using predicate calculus (e.g. Gentner, 1983). Relations are predicates taking two or more arguments, such as COLLIDE (x,y). "Higher-order" relations are two-or-more-place predicates, such as CAUSE [COLLIDE (x,y), STRIKE (y,z)]. Attributes are predicates taking one argument, such as LARGE (x).

However, predicate structure also represents choices made by the theorist, who makes the important decisions about syntactic parsing. Predicate structure does not necessarily provide a way of distinguishing between relations with psychological significance. For example, the "higher-order" relation CAUSE [PUSH (object 1, object 2), COLLIDE (object 1, object 2)] can also be represented as CAUSE-TO-COLLIDE-BY-PUSHING [intended to be a new, single concept] (object 1, object 2), a representation that does not distinguish it as "higher-order" (Palmer, 1989). Once again, the "lower-order" or "higher-order" status of the relations is arbitrary unless we have an independent way of defining what the basic concepts are.

*Relational Knowledge and Relational Similarity*

The distinction that these descriptions of the relations in an analogy seek to represent is actually quite simple. It is the distinction between the child's knowledge that the relations in the two halves of any analogy must be similar, and his or her knowledge about how the objects in an analogy are related. In this book, I will refer to the need to equate the relations in each half of an analogy as the *relational similarity constraint*. The "lower-order" relations that must be equated in order to fulfil this constraint will be referred to simply as *relations*. According to my representational choices, a child's ability to recognise and to use the relational similarity constraint becomes the "hallmark" of analogical reasoning.

To illustrate, consider some of the analogies that we have been discussing. These include the classical analogies *food:body::rain:ground* and *nurse:syringe::barber:scissors*, and the problem analogy about the genie rolling up his carpet and the child rolling up some paper. The *relations* in these analogies include knowledge about how rain nurtures the ground and how food fuels the body, knowledge about the tools of different trades, and knowledge about rolling up paper and rolling up carpets. To solve analogies based on these relations, however, children must apply the *relational similarity constraint*. The relations between the objects in the base and the target in a problem analogy, and the relations linking the A and the B terms and the C and the D terms in a classical analogy, must be chosen to be similar. By this account, the test of structural theories of analogical development becomes a test of children's use of the relational similarity constraint. However, a consideration of the second assumption mentioned earlier shows that this test may not be a straightforward one.

## 2. The Assumption of Knowledge

The second assumption on which structural theory was based is that younger children know the relations necessary to solve the analogies that they are being tested with. This assumption is central to the interpretation of analogical performance. If a child knows the relations on which an analogy is based and yet fails to apply the relational similarity constraint, then this child would be performing in line with structural theory. However, if the child does not understand the relations in a given analogy and fails to apply the relational similarity constraint, then no conclusions about competence can be drawn. A child cannot equate relations that he or she does not know or understand.

For example, consider once again the classical analogy *food:body::rain:* (water, storm, coat, *ground*). If a child knows that food nurtures the body and that rain nurtures the ground, then he or she should be able to solve the analogy by equating the relations between the A:B and the C:D terms, unless other factors intervene. However, if a child knows that food nurtures the body but not that rain nurtures the ground, then he or she will be unable to solve the analogy by equating the relations between the A:B and the C:D terms. Similarly, if a child knows that nurses use syringes but not that barbers use scissors, then he or she may well complete the Piagetian analogy *nurse:syringe::barber:* ? with the D term "washbasin". In either case, it would be impossible to measure that child's *capacity* to use the relational similarity constraint, because the child would have insufficient knowledge of the relations that he or she was required to equate.

The same argument applies to solving problem analogies. Children must know and understand the relations between objects in the base and objects in the target in order to recognise similarities between these relations. Problem analogy researchers have been more aware of this requirement, and have tried to use very simple relations in their experiments with children. However, the problem analogy paradigm can be vulnerable to a different problem: Children will frequently fail to notice the relational correspondences set up by the experimenters. After all, they do not know that they are being tested for their ability to apply analogies. Their apparent task is to solve a problem that they have been given, and in these circumstances they will often ignore relational correspondences that it is a fair bet that they understand. This leads us to the third assumption underlying structural theory, which is that the child is aware of the analogical goal of equating relations.

## 3. The Assumption of "Meta-knowledge"

Even if younger children know the relations on which an analogy is based, they may fail to solve that analogy because they do not realise that they need to seek relational similarities. For example, in Holyoak et al.'s task, the younger children apparently failed to notice the potential similarity between a genie magically commanding his carpet to roll itself into a tube, and their own possible actions with a sheet of paper. This failure occurred even though the children were probably very familiar with the fact that sheets of paper can be rolled up. So in problem analogy experiments, one difficulty is that children may fail to apply the appropriate relational focus. This again raises difficulties for the interpretation of their analogical performance. A failure to seek relational correspondence is not necessarily the same thing as an inability to use the relational similarity constraint.

In classical analogy experiments, a failure to realise that the goal is to seek relational similarity will also lead to poor performance, even if a child knows all the relations in the analogy. Children who are unaware of the importance of the relational similarity constraint may choose one relation to link the A and the B terms, and another to link the C and the D terms, reasoning *successively* about the relations in the analogy. Again, we would be reluctant to say that such failures were competence-based. To provide an adequate test of structural theory, it must thus be ensured that the child understands the nature of the analogy task as well as the relations involved in the analogy. If the child understands the analogical goal of equating relations and yet is incapable of doing so until a certain developmental stage is reached, then this would provide better support for the idea of an age-related shift in analogical reasoning.

## KNOWLEDGE-BASED ACCOUNTS OF ANALOGICAL REASONING

An alternative account of analogical development is a knowledge-based one. This account proposes that the depth of a child's conceptual knowledge will play an important role in that child's analogical reasoning. According to knowledge-based theories, if the appropriate relations in a conceptual domain have already been worked out, then children should be able to make analogies based on those relations. Knowledge-based accounts of analogical development have been put forward by a number of authors (e.g. Brown, 1989; Gentner, 1989; Goswami, 1989; Goswami & Brown, 1989; Vosniadou, 1989). These researchers broadly argue that apparent shifts in analogical reasoning with age reflect the growing knowledge of the young child. Most of the accounts propose that even very young children have the capacity to reason about relational similarity, but that this ability can be masked by a lack of relational knowledge.

The main difference between knowledge-based views of analogical development and structural views is that the former do not predict age-related shifts in the ability to reason by analogy. Knowledge-based views do predict age-related improvements in analogical reasoning, as children will be able to solve more analogies as they acquire more knowledge, but they do not predict global shifts. However, it is important to be clear that knowledge-based accounts do not predict that children will always reason by analogy if they have the appropriate relational knowledge, or that younger children's analogical performance will be equivalent to that of older children in such cases. Children of all ages may fail to reason by analogy for a variety of reasons that are not related to competence, but that still affect performance. The contrast with structural theory is that these other factors can all be clearly specified.

For example, some children may be more easily distracted by extraneous task factors than other children. They may also be less likely to think of using an analogy when one is appropriate, or they may be less likely to notice when an analogy is appropriate. Such performance factors may cause differences in the number of analogies solved by different children of the same age, or by younger and older children who possess the same relational knowledge. Knowledge-based views can thus accommodate differences in analogical performance with age. The important difference is that knowledge-based theories do not predict an age-related shift in analogical development, whereas structural theories do.

## The Relational Difficulty Hypothesis

In this book, I will argue for an extreme version of the knowledge-based view. My argument will be that the ability to recognise relational similarity may not develop at all. Children may be able to recognise relational similarity at any point in development, even from the very first months of life. Their ability to do so will depend on the difficulty of the relations on which the analogy is based. When the relations in the analogy have been worked out and represented conceptually, then children should be able to apply the relational similarity constraint, unless performance factors intervene. If the relations are not worked out or understood, then children's ability to recognise relational similarity will be hidden. So if the relations in an analogy are already part of conceptual knowledge, then recognising their similarity should not constitute an extra cognitive load.

This *relational difficulty hypothesis* is based on the idea that the constraint on the development of analogical reasoning is the recognition or discovery of relationships in the developing knowledge base, rather than the recognition and use of relational similarity itself. Relations can only be recognised as similar when they are represented as part of the child's growing knowledge about the world, and whereas it can be argued that perceptual knowledge is inherently structured, conceptual knowledge is not. Children need to structure their increasing conceptual knowledge about the world in a way that represents fundamental principles and causal relationships. Analogical reasoning provides an especially stringent test of their ability to achieve this, as a clear understanding of the relationships that hold within a given conceptual domain is required in order to solve analogies set within that domain. This is probably why analogical reasoning skills are a good correlate of I.Q., as more difficult analogies require a deeper understanding of the relationships that hold within any domain.

The relational difficulty hypothesis makes a number of predictions, and these will be examined in the chapters that follow. The first is that the apparent evidence for an age-related shift in analogical reasoning should turn out to be artefactual. The widely-documented failure of younger children to use the relational similarity constraint when solving classical analogies should turn out to be a function of relational difficulty. Evidence relevant to this prediction will be considered in Chapters 2 and 3.

The second prediction is that in the absence of relational knowledge, or when only partial relational knowledge is present, then children will resort to other kinds of reasoning strategies in analogy tasks. Because their relational knowledge is insufficient for analogy, they will not use the relational similarity constraint as a basis for solution. Instead, they may reason about other kinds of similarity, such as perceptual similarity, or they may reason about other kinds of relations, such as associative ones. The evidence relating to this prediction is considered in Chapters 3, 4 and 5.

The third prediction is that, unless performance factors intervene, children who do have the appropriate relational knowledge should find it easy to use the relational similarity constraint to solve analogies. Even babies should be sensitive to relational similarity if they have represented the appropriate relations conceptually, or if the relations that are similar are perceptual rather than conceptual ones. The recognition of relational similarity may be an inherent quality of human reasoning, one that is applied whenever some of the relations between objects in a new domain are understood. We have seen that scientific discovery can depend on the recognition of relational similarity, and babies are somewhat similar to experimental scientists in the strategies that they use to acquire knowledge (e.g. Harris, 1983). The recognition of relational similarity could be an inherent quality of human reasoning *even if* meta-knowledge of the relational similarity constraint does not emerge until later in development (see also Halford, in press).

If this idea about the importance of analogy in knowledge acquisition is correct, then it should be possible to show that relational similarity is used spontaneously by infants who are learning about their worlds, and by young children who are acquiring knowledge in their classrooms. As we will see in Chapters 6 and 7, there is a growing body of evidence that suggests that this is indeed the case. Children frequently use analogies to develop their theories about the world, just as Kepler used an analogy to develop his theory about celestial mechanics. However, the use of analogy will interact with the degree of knowledge that a child has about the relations within a conceptual domain, as it did with Kepler. To begin making analogies that will extend knowledge, a certain amount of data is required in the first place.

# CHAPTER TWO

# Structural Theories of the Development of Analogical Reasoning

I argued in the last chapter that the ability to recognise relational similarity may not develop, in which case the evidence for an age-related shift in analogical reasoning should turn out to be an artefact of relational difficulty. This in fact seems to be the case. The age-related shift, which seemed to occur in early adolescence, was first documented by Piaget and his colleagues (Inhelder & Piaget, 1958; Piaget et al., 1977). To see why the belief in this age-related shift was so widespread, we must re-examine the evidence for Piaget's structural theory of analogical development in some detail.

## PIAGET'S THEORY OF ANALOGICAL REASONING

Piaget's view of mental development was a constructivist one. He believed that there were global changes in all kinds of logical reasoning with development. Adolescents reasoned in qualitatively different ways from younger children, who in turn reasoned in qualitatively different ways from infants. There were two major changes in the development of logical reasoning in childhood, which occurred at around 7 and 11 years. These ages marked respectively the onset of *concrete-operational reasoning*, when children began to use mental operations such as transitivity and class inclusion, and the onset of *formal-operational reasoning*, when children became able to take the results of concrete operations (such as which objects belonged in a particular class) and generate hypotheses about their logical relationships (such as the possible relations between these classes).

The major changes in the development of analogical reasoning were thought to correspond to these two stages of concrete operations and formal operations. The ability to reason about relations first emerged at the age of around 7 years, when children became able to solve class inclusion problems. The ability to construct classes meant that the children could now reason about how the objects in the classes were related. Once children appreciated how objects were related, they became able to construct relations *between* these relations, enabling the emergence of "higher-order" relational reasoning at around 11–12 years. At this point, the ability to reason about the relational similarity constraint emerged. Prior to understanding the relational similarity constraint, children had only a *successive* understanding of the relations in analogies.

## Piaget's Task

To test this theory, Piaget et al. (1977) designed an ingenious pictorial version of the classical analogy task. In the first stage of the task, children were asked to sort through a set of pictures. After establishing that the children could recognise the objects shown in the pictures (e.g. a dog, a ship, a vacuum cleaner, a feather, a ship's helm, an electric plug), the experimenter asked the children to "put together the pictures that go well together". Most children sorted the pictures into pairs. In the second stage of the task, the children were asked to make these pairs into foursomes. They were told that the foursomes "must go well together". Following this second sort, the children were asked to justify their selection of particular pairs and foursomes (analogies).

Many of the children did not find the second stage of creating analogies at all easy. For these children, Piaget and his colleagues provided a series of graded hints about the relations in the analogies. For example, for the analogy *bird:feathers::dog:hair*, the experimenter would ask "What keeps the bird warm in winter? Feathers". If the child still failed to recognise that the *dog* and its *hair* were the appropriate matching pair, then the experimenter would hint at the relational similarity constraint. Placing the picture of the dog beneath that of the bird, the experimenter would indicate the empty cell of this 2 x 2 picture matrix, and would ask "What would go well here? It must be something which is for the dog as the feathers are for the bird". If the child still failed to form an analogy after these prompts, he or she was shown three alternative pictures that could fill the empty cell, and was asked to choose between them.

Once the analogy was formed, the experimenter would propose alternative completion terms (D terms) as a further test of whether the children really understood the relational similarity constraint. Piaget called these alternative solutions "counter-suggestions". For example, the experimenter might ask whether a picture of a *kennel* would be as good as the picture of *hair* in the analogy *bird:feathers::dog:hair*, or whether a picture of a *bell* or a *bicycle pump* would be as good as the picture of the *handlebars* in the analogy *ship:helm::bicycle:handlebars*. In addition to being asked to judge the acceptability of these counter-suggestions, older children were presented with completed analogies, and were asked to justify the selection of the terms in them. Again, Piaget et al. wanted to examine the children's understanding of the relational similarity constraint.

## Piaget's Stages of Analogical Development

From the children's performance in these tasks, Piaget and his colleagues identified three different stages in the development of analogical reasoning. These stages fitted neatly with Piaget's general theory of mental development. Stage I corresponded to the Piagetian stage of pre-operational reasoning, and was typically found at age 5–6 years. Stage II corresponded to the stage of concrete operational reasoning, and extended from 7–8 years to 10–11 years. Stage III corresponded to the formal-operational stage of reasoning, and emerged at 11–12 years.

*Stage I*
Performance at Stage I was characterised by complete failure in both components of analogical reasoning. During this stage, children were unable to recognise either the relations between the pictures or the relational similarity constraint. Instead of sorting the pictures by causal relations and relational similarity, they used a variety of different strategies, strategies which Piaget argued were quite idiosyncratic.

For example, Cou. (aged 5 years, 3 months) sorted the pairs of pictures by similarity of appearance (*vacuum cleaner–ship:* "because it looks like a ship"), by association (*ship–bird:* "because the bird is sometimes on the lake") and by causal connections (*vacuum cleaner–feather:* "because it hoovers up the feather"). When asked to complete the 2 x 2 matrices, Cou. appeared completely bewildered. For example, offered the grouping *bird:feather::dog:?*, Cou. said that a picture of a dog's lead was required, and when given the alternatives *car, dog hairs, vacuum cleaner*, she chose the car "because the dog sometimes rides in the car". This "egocentric" reasoning was said to be typical of children in the first part of Stage I, Stage IA.

Cou. did show analogical reasoning with one 2 x 2 matrix, and this was the analogy *bicycle:handlebars::ship:helm*. Here she told the experimenter that the handlebars were the steering of the bicycle, and the helm was the steering of the ship: "the steering wheel is what one uses for driving and the handlebars, c'est la meme chose". However, Piaget argued that her understanding of this analogy was only momentary, and so did not constitute analogical reasoning. Cou. would willingly accept other pairings for the same objects.

The second part of Stage I, Stage IB, was marked by an increasing stability in the children's relational choices. Most of the relations in Piaget's analogies were causal ones, and Can. (aged 5 years, 8 months) paired many of the pictures by cause–effect relations, for example *vacuum cleaner–plug* ("else one can't hoover"), *helm–ship* ("to steer the ship"), *dog–hairs* ("otherwise it feels cold"). However, Can. was apparently unable to use the relational similarity constraint to group these pairs of pictures into analogies. For example, when given the 2 x 2 matrices, he selected *car–petrol* to match *bicycle–handlebars* (as both were "for going on the road"). Explaining the analogy *bird:feathers::dog:hair*, he said that the pictures belonged together because "the dog eats the bird, those are the feathers!"

By the end of Stage I, the children thus showed an emerging ability to reason about relations, but showed no understanding of the relational similarity constraint. This emergent understanding of relations was said to be fragile, however. The children could always think of a variety of idiosyncratic reasons for relating the pictures, other than the intended causal relations. According to Piaget, the children were pairing the objects by essentially variable properties: by associations, by similarities in appearance, by part–whole relationships, and so on. This variability meant that they could not sort the objects into the fixed framework of classes and sub-classes that was thought to be necessary for a true apprehension of relations. Piaget noted that such variability in reasoning was characteristic of the egocentric child.

*Stage II*
Piaget's second stage in the development of analogical reasoning, which coincided with the onset of concrete operations, was marked by an increasing ability to reason about relations, and by an emerging ability to recognise the relational similarity constraint.

This second stage was also divided into two parts. In Stage IIA, the children could successfully form analogies by trial and error, but showed no evidence of understanding the relational similarity constraint. Their lack of understanding was demonstrated by their willingness to accept counter-suggestions that destroyed the analogies. For example, Bol.

(aged 6 years, 6 months) put the picture pair *ship–helm* with *bicycle–handlebars*, "for steering", but then accepted the counter-suggestion *pump*, "Yes, to pump it up" [the bicycle tyre]. Mag. (aged 6 years, 9 months) matched the picture pair *dog–hairs* with *bird–feathers* "because they are both animals", and paired *ship–helm* with *bicycle–handlebars*, but also later accepted the *pump* as a replacement for the handlebars "to blow up the tyres". Cyn. (aged 7 years, 6 months) completed the matrix *eyes:television::ears:radio*, but then accepted the *plug* in place of the eyes.

This willingness to accept counter-suggestions was theoretically very important. Piaget argued that it showed that the children were only capable of thinking about the relations in the analogies in *successive* terms. Although their growing ability to construct stable classes of objects (the "consolidation of elementary relations") frequently enabled them to work out the analogies correctly by trial and error, Piaget argued that this ability was only a preliminary for true analogical reasoning. The children still described the relations in their analogies consecutively rather than by reference to the relational similarity constraint, which was evidence that they lacked a true understanding of analogy.

For example, when Mur. (aged 7 years, 9 months) was asked to explain the analogy *nurse:syringe::barber:scissors*, she replied that the pairs of pictures went together because the syringe and the scissors were utensils, and the nurse and the barber were occupations. When explaining the analogy *bicycle:handlebars::ship:helm*, she said that handlebars and helms were for steering, and ships and bicycles were both means of transport. For the analogy *bird:feathers::dog:hairs*, she said that the bird and the dog were both animals, and that the hair and the feathers were "like a blanket for us". The example that Piaget gives here does not really seem to support his theory. Although it is true that Mur. does not refer to the relational similarity constraint in her explanations, she is describing the relations between the A and the C terms and the B and the D terms rather than the relations between A and B, or C and D. This implies a deeper understanding of analogy than simply reporting successive associations.

In the later half of Stage II, Stage IIB, the children in Piaget's study became able to reject the counter-suggestions. They had apparently achieved the critical insight that the successful completion of the matrices depended on the relation between A and B being the *same* as that between C and D. However, in spite of their apparent understanding of the relational similarity constraint, they still formed analogies by a process of trial and error. Piaget argued that children in Stage II were not yet able to operate *mentally* on the relations in the analogies. The ability to imagine analogies—to construct them without any concrete feedback—had still to emerge in Stage III.

## Stage III

Entry into Stage III marked complete understanding of the relational similarity constraint, and coincided with the onset of Piagetian formal-operational reasoning. The trial-and-error construction of analogies dropped out, and the children became able to justify their solutions in terms of relational similarity. They also consistently rejected counter-suggestions from the experimenter that destroyed the analogies. So in the formal-operational stage, the children were finally able to work out analogies by mentally constructing the relations in them in accordance with the relational similarity constraint.

## Evaluation

How far should we accept Piaget's conclusions about analogical development? At least three important claims can be identified in Piaget's structural theory, all of which require further documentation. The first claim, and the most striking, is that children are unable to reason about the relational similarity constraint* until they reach adolescence. This claim has been very influential. It is the basis of the widespread view that analogy is a sophisticated form of reasoning that has a late onset.

The second claim is that the ability to reason about relations develops separately from, and prior to, the ability to reason about relational similarity. For Piaget, these were qualitatively different kinds of reasoning, and required different skills. Reasoning about relations depended on the ability to construct classes of objects. Reasoning about the relational similarity constraint also grew out of the ability to construct classes, but represented a later stage of higher-order class relationships, and was in addition said to be connected to the ability to reason about proportions (as we shall see).

The third claim concerns the role of counter-suggestions. These were thought to provide a test of the children's understanding of the relational similarity constraint, which the counter-suggestions violated. However, to demonstrate an understanding of relational similarity by rejecting counter-suggestions, the children had to disagree with the experimenters. Younger children may have been more reluctant to disagree with adults than older children, and so this may not have been an appropriate test of their understanding, although it is an intriguing one. Of these three claims, the one that initially stimulated the most developmental research was Piaget's idea that analogical reasoning was a formal-operational skill.

## PIAGET'S CLAIMS

### 1. The Formal-Operational Claim

An interesting aspect of much of the research based on Piaget's first claim was that it often produced contradictory results. Many researchers found that children *could* solve analogies prior to the formal-operational period. However, this evidence for an early analogical capacity was usually dismissed as being spurious. Researchers in the Piagetian tradition were convinced that there should be a qualitative change in analogical reasoning at around 11–12 years of age.

For example, Gallagher and Wright (1979) gave children aged 9–12 years two different kinds of written verbal analogies to solve. One kind was based on what the authors called "concrete" relations, such as the analogy *"Picture* is related to *Frame* as *Yard* is to: Swings, Tree, Children, *Fence"*. Gallagher and Wright argued that "concrete" analogies could be solved by attending to "directly observable features of content". The other kind was based on so-called "abstract" relations, such as the analogy *"Food* is related to *Body* as *Rain* is to: Water, Storm, Coat, *Ground"*. For these analogies, "solution seemed to be based upon a movement beyond observable features to a higher-order rule" (p. 116). In other words, to solve the "abstract" analogies, the children had to have extra knowledge about how food and the body were related, information that was not directly observable. They needed to have worked out certain conceptual relationships.

Gallagher and Wright found that while the 9- and 10-year-old children in their study could solve the concrete analogies, successful performance with the abstract analogies showed a big increase at around age 12. They concluded that this shift in performance confirmed Piaget's theory of analogical development. Although the younger children were successfully solving the concrete analogies, Gallagher and Wright argued that they could solve them without using the relational similarity constraint. Their apparent analogical skills could be based on associative reasoning. For example, the concrete analogy *"Picture* is related to *Frame* as *Yard* is to: Swings, Tree, Children, *Fence"* could be solved on the basis of the strong association between yard and fence, without using the relational similarity constraint. No independent evidence for this associative explanation was offered, however, and it was entirely *post hoc.*

Gallagher and Wright's negative conclusion about the younger children's ability was all the more surprising because they were among the first researchers to note the importance of making a distinction between form (the structure of the analogy) and content (the relations that the children were required to reason about) in explaining analogical development. However, Gallagher and Wright were not making a knowledge-based argument. By "content", they meant the *kind* of relations supporting solution (associative *vs* analogical), rather than whether the child possessed the appropriate relational knowledge. As responses based on associative reasoning and responses based on the relational similarity constraint were identical in their experiment, however, we cannot tell whether the children were using associative reasoning as a substitute for analogical reasoning or not. Furthermore, the relations in the abstract analogies (e.g. nurturing) required more conceptual knowledge on the part of the child than those in the concrete analogies. This could also explain the shift in performance found at age 12—the older children may have had greater relational knowledge.

Dismissals of early competence as being due to associative reasoning are very frequent in the literature, however. Many researchers in the Piagetian tradition have made claims similar to those of Gallagher and Wright. These explanations of early competence are based on the assumption that the correct answer to the analogy is selected on the basis of an associative relationship between C and D. The implication is that the relationship between A and B is ignored. Notice that the children in Gallagher and Wright's experiment would have selected the *same* associative answers if they were using the relational similarity constraint, however. They may even have been trying to equate associative relations (i.e. reasoning that B is an associate of A, and so therefore D should be an associate of C). To distinguish properly between analogical and associative reasoning, we need to design analogies in which the correct solution to the analogy is not also an associative response.

An experiment by Levinson and Carpenter (1974) is relevant here. They designed a series of classical analogies in which the D term was a word that was associated with the C term less than 8% of the time according to word-association norms. They also chose analogy items that were certain to be in the children's vocabularies. A typical analogy would be "*Bird* is to *air* as *fish* is to ? (*water*)". In a control condition, the children were given the same analogies in a format that presented them with the correct relations and that also removed the need to use the relational similarity constraint. These control items were called "quasi-analogies". The quasi-analogy for "*Bird* is to *air* as *fish* is to ? (*water*)" would be "A bird flies in the air; a fish swims in the ?". So the quasi-analogies simply tested the children's relational knowledge. According to structural theory, younger children should succeed in solving the quasi-analogies and fail with the "true" analogies, because the relational similarity constraint is only required to solve the true analogies.

In their experiment, Levinson and Carpenter gave groups of children aged 9, 12 and 15 years both types of analogy to solve. Half of the children were given the quasi-analogies first, and half were given the true analogies first. In line with Piagetian theory, the 9-year-olds were significantly better at solving the quasi-analogies than the true analogies, whereas the 12- and the 15-year-olds performed equally well with both types. Levinson and Carpenter concluded that the two older groups did have "an ability which contributed to their facility to solve verbal analogies which was more developed than that of the 9-year-old subjects" (p. 859). They thought that this ability could relate to "the type and number of relationships between word pairs which 9-year-old subjects could consider"—in other words, to their relational knowledge.

It is simple to test this explanation. If the younger children's poorer performance with the true analogies was a function of their relational knowledge, then a transfer effect should have been found. Children who received the quasi-analogies first should have shown better performance with the true analogies than children who received the true analogies first, since the quasi-analogies provided the children with the correct relational knowledge to solve the true analogies. Such a transfer effect was indeed found. This suggests that the degree of a child's relational knowledge did play an important role in their ability to solve the true analogies. Even 9-year-olds (children in the concrete-operational stage of reasoning) had the competence to reason by analogy in this experiment.

However, some Piagetians would argue that the kind of analogies used by Levinson and Carpenter did not enable a true test of Piaget's theory. Lunzer (1965) proposed that these kinds of verbal analogies, which he called "Type A" analogies (his example was "*Leather* is to *shoe* as *wool* is to ?"), could be solved by "reading off" the relation between the A and the B terms and applying it to the C term. In his view, such "reading off" required only simple classification skills—a concrete reasoning ability.

Lunzer contrasted Type A analogies with more complex "Type D" analogies, such as "*Leather* is to *soft/shoe/hide* as *hard/clay/house* is to *brick*". He argued that Type D analogies did require formal-operational reasoning. In these analogies, the children had not only to recognise the relation required to solve the analogy, but also its *direction*. *Leather* is the raw material for *shoes*, and so by analogy *clay* is the raw material for *bricks*: the response *house* (based on the relation that bricks are the raw material for houses) is in the wrong direction.

According to our definition of analogy, both Type A analogies and Type D analogies require children to use the relational similarity constraint. The relation that is "read off" in the Type A analogies still has to be equated for both halves of the analogy. So Lunzer's claim that only Type D analogies enable a proper test of Piaget's theory would not seem to be correct. However, it is probably true that the Type D analogies are more difficult for younger children to solve, as they make greater performance demands—for example, they contain more information for the children to process, and so there is a greater memory load. Thus an age-related shift in performance with the Type A and the Type D analogies may be found despite the fact that both types of analogy involve the relational similarity constraint.

Lunzer's results confirmed the difficulty of the Type D analogies. He tested 153 boys aged from 9 to 18 years, and found that none of the 9-year-olds could reach a criterion of 3/4 correct on the easiest Type D items. In contrast, 45% of the 11-year-olds reached this criterion. With the Type A analogies, 18% of the 9-year-olds were able to reach criterion (5/8 analogies solved correctly), compared to 80% of the 11-year-olds. So there was an age-related shift in analogical reasoning.

However, the performance of the 9-year-olds was much poorer than would be predicted if the Type A analogies required only concrete-operational reasoning. This convinced Lunzer that even these "elementary" analogies required formal-operational reasoning levels. He concluded that whereas tasks such as series completion (e.g. 3, 6, 9, 12, ?) required the continuation of a lower-order relation (such as the repeated addition of a constant number—a concrete-operational skill), analogies required the use of the relational similarity constraint, and this skill was only found in formal-operational children.

Lunzer's study is frequently quoted as providing strong support for Piaget's structural model of analogical development. The rather striking change at age 11 in the percentage of children able to solve the Type A analogies (from 18% to 80%) is in line with the predictions of structural theory. However, Lunzer's data are completely ambiguous, because we do not know about relational difficulty. If the younger boys did not understand the relation between, for example, *shoes* and *leather*, or *cardigans* (sweaters) and *wool*, then they would be unable to demonstrate the so-called "higher level" of reasoning required to use the relational similarity constraint. The older boys' success with Lunzer's analogies may simply have been due to their greater knowledge of the relevant relations.

## 2. The "Proportional Reasoning" Claim

Another source of evidence for the idea that a higher level of reasoning was required in order to use the relational similarity constraint was the widespread belief that Inhelder and Piaget (1958) had claimed that analogies involved proportions. Proportional reasoning was meant to be a hallmark of formal-operational reasoning. It therefore followed that if analogies required proportional reasoning, then analogical reasoning required formal-operational skills. For example, Lunzer argued that the logical structure of an analogy like *leather:shoe::wool:cardigan* was equivalent to a proportional expression like 3:4 = 15:20. Many other authors in the Piagetian tradition have expressed similar views (e.g. Levinson & Carpenter, 1974; Gallagher & Wright, 1977, 1979). Despite this consensus, however, Inhelder and Piaget's actual beliefs about the connection between analogical and proportional reasoning are not very clear. They wrote:

> Mathematical proportions consist simply of the equality of two ratios, $x/y = x'/y'$. Their formulation raises a psychological problem only because it does not take place during the concrete operational stage. The subject at this level can already construct fractions ... moreover ... beginning with the concrete level, we see evidence of what Spearman has called 'the education of correlates' in which the subject formulates the links in a double-entry table in such a way as to forecast proportions: for example, 'Rome is to Italy as Paris is to France'. This is why we wonder why the 8–11 year old subjects are not able to discover the equality of two ratios which form a proportion ... (p. 314).

Although Inhelder and Piaget thought that analogical reasoning and proportional reasoning were related, this statement does not seem to predict a strong link between analogical and proportional reasoning. In fact, Piaget later apparently solved the problem of the late emergence of proportional reasoning by placing the full emergence of analogical reasoning in the formal-operational period as well (Piaget et al., 1977).

*Measuring Proportional Reasoning*
Despite the lack of clarity in Piaget's position about analogies and proportions, the supposed link between analogical reasoning and proportional reasoning has provided an alternative way for researchers to assess children's understanding of the relational similarity constraint. Many authors have simply assumed that one ability (proportional reasoning) provides an index of the other (analogical reasoning), and have set out to devise different ways of measuring proportional understanding.

For example, Gallagher and Wright (1977) investigated the link between the development of what they described as "symmetrical" (proportional) reasoning and analogy. They argued that analogical responses could either be symmetrical (demonstrating an "awareness of total structure") or asymmetrical (demonstrating a "failure to compare both sides of the analogy, or to balance both sides", p. 6). Only symmetrical responses showed an understanding of proportionality. For example, in the analogy "*Automobile* is related to *Gas* as *Sailboat* is to: Travel, *Wind*, Sails, Rudder", a symmetrical response would be "An automobile gets its energy to go from gas and a sailboat from wind. They both need something to make them go". An asymmetrical response would be "You need a rudder for the boat", or "You put gas in a car and sail a sailboat when it is windy".

Gallagher and Wright gave children aged from 9 to 12 years a series of 15 such verbal analogies to solve, presented in a written multiple-choice format. The children were required to give written explanations of their answers, which were then scored for evidence of symmetrical responding. The results showed an increase in such symmetrical responding with age, and a corresponding increase in the number of analogies solved successfully. Gallagher and Wright then showed that, even after controlling for I.Q., symmetrical responding was a significant predictor of analogical performance in a multiple regression. So the two measures did seem to be related. Maybe this was not surprising, as "symmetrical responses" in this experiment were basically a description of the relational similarity constraint.

In the study mentioned earlier, Levinson and Carpenter also examined the degree to which an understanding of proportional relationships might influence successful analogical performance. They asked four children from each of the age groups that they tested to provide explanations for their "true analogy" responses. These explanations were then scored for evidence of proportional understanding. To be counted as demonstrating proportional understanding, an explanation had to describe the relationships both within and between each part of the analogy. For example, for the analogy *foot:inches::minute:seconds*, a child who said "The inches in a foot are segments; you told me that, so I gave you the segments that are in a minute" (p. 858) was scored as understanding proportionality.

The number of proportional responses that the children in Levinson and Carpenter's study produced was found to increase significantly with age. There was also a relationship between the ability to provide proportional explanations and successful analogical responding. Levinson and Carpenter concluded that an understanding of proportionality may have contributed to analogical success. However, once again the measure of proportional understanding was basically the ability to describe the relational similarity constraint. This measure of proportional understanding is very different from Piaget's criterion of an equality of two ratios, $x/y$ and $x'/y'$. So the relationship that Levinson and Carpenter found between their two measures takes us no further in deciding whether reasoning about relational similarity is related to proportionality and may therefore require a "higher level" of reasoning.

The only study that has investigated this relationship by using a measure of proportional understanding that is independent of the analogy measure is the study by Lunzer (1965), which was also described earlier. He asked his subjects to solve "numerical analogies" as well as verbal analogies. The numerical analogies were geometric series problems involving proportionality, such as 3:1, 9:7, 10:8, 4: ? (the relation is to subtract 2 from the first number); 8:17, 4:9, 3:7, ?:6 (the relation is 1/2[x – 1]); and 5:125, 4:64, 2:8, 3: ? (the relation is to cube the first number).

The boys in Lunzer's study found these problems very difficult. The percentage of problems solved successfully by at least 40% of the children was 0% for the 9- to 10-year-old age group, 6% for the 10- to 11-year-old age group, and 44% for the 11- to 12-year-old age group. Lunzer concluded that the shift in performance at age 11 was further evidence that analogies required a more complex reasoning process than was available prior to adolescence. The finding that performance with both the verbal and the numerical analogies showed a shift at the same age seemed to be evidence that children's difficulty with analogies involved reasoning about proportional relations, and that both abilities were formal-operational skills.

However, the relational difficulty confound that we noted earlier also applies to Lunzer's mathematical data. Some of the arithmetical operations required to solve the numerical analogies are quite difficult. For example, the younger boys may not have been very good at calculating fractions or at cubing numbers. Therefore, they may have performed poorly with the numerical analogies because of a lack of mathematical knowledge, and not because of the proportional structure of these problems. So the question of whether there is a connection between analogical reasoning and proportional reasoning remains open.

## 3. The Role of Counter-suggestions

Piaget's third theoretical claim concerned the role of counter-suggestions in the development of analogical reasoning. Counter-suggestions were meant to provide a further means of testing children's understanding of the relational similarity constraint. As the counter-suggestions were chosen to violate this constraint, it was expected that children who understood the relational similarity constraint would reject the counter-suggestions. Piaget found that most children did not do this consistently until they had reached the formal-operational period. This was taken as evidence that the younger children's understanding of the relations involved in analogy was successive in nature, and did not involve relational similarity.

However, there is an obvious problem with Piaget's questioning technique, which is that the younger children may not have liked to contradict the experimenter. The older children may have been more confident, enabling them to reject the counter-suggestions and so demonstrate their understanding of relational similarity. We need to devise a way of using counter-suggestions that is not vulnerable to such social constraints.

One way is to use the multiple-choice technique, and to include counter-suggestions as some of the distractors. This approach was used by Gallagher and Wright in their 1977 study. For example, in their analogy "*Automobile* is related to *Gas* as *Sailboat* is to Travel, *Wind*, Sails, Rudder", the incorrect response "Sails" was the counter-suggestion. They found that the younger children (9-year-olds) tended to select the counter-suggestions rather than the correct responses to complete their analogies. For example, for the analogy "*Food:Body* as *Rain:*Water, Storm, Coat, *Ground*", the counter-suggestion "Water" was the response that the younger children selected most frequently.

Once again, however, we have to worry about relational difficulty. Children may only choose counter-suggestions when they do not know the relations on which the analogies are based. As counter-suggestions are frequently high associates of the C term, children might select an associative relation whenever they do not know the relevant analogical relation. If this were the case, then a preference for counter-suggestions would not be evidence for an inability to understand the relational similarity constraint.

It is also possible that in some cases the children thought that the counter-suggestions in Gallagher and Wright's analogies *did* fulfil the relational similarity constraint. Some of the explanations that the children came up with when they chose the counter-suggestions as responses makes this quite plausible. For example, in the "*Food:Body* as *Rain:*(*Ground*/Water)" analogy, the children who selected the counter-suggestion "Water" gave explanations such as "Food goes down the body and water goes down as rain". The relation "goes down" was thus used in both parts of the analogy, fulfilling the relational similarity constraint. So the children might have been choosing associative solutions on the *basis* of relational similarity.

Another way of testing Piaget's idea that the choice of counter-suggestions shows a failure to understand the relational similarity constraint is to look for other evidence that younger children prefer to use associations when solving analogies. A preference for associative solutions would provide converging evidence that younger children have a successive understanding of the relations in analogies (counter-suggestions are usually high associates of the C term). However, in order to establish an associative preference, it is crucial to ensure that the children know the relations on which the analogies are based. If younger children cannot use the relational similarity constraint, then they should prefer associative responses even when they have sufficient relational knowledge to solve the analogy. Of course, even then it remains possible that they show this preference because they do not realise that relational similarity is relevant.

### Associative Responding vs Analogical Reasoning

The possibility that classical analogies can be correctly solved by associative reasoning without any need to use relational similarity has long interested psychometricians. For example, Gentile and his co-workers found that much of the variance in adult performance on the analogy items in standardised I.Q. tests could be accounted for by an "associative mechanism" (identified in terms of the relatedness of the C and the D terms). Gentile also showed experimentally that manipulating the degree of association between the B and the C terms could affect responding in classical analogies. For example, when adult subjects were asked to solve analogies of the form *FIRE:ASHES*:: 1. winter:ice, 2. tree:leaves, 3. Christmas:holly, 4. *event:memories*, the semantic associations between *fires, ashes, leaves* and *trees* turned out to be more potent in determining solution than the analogical relation between *fire:ashes* and *event:memories* (Gentile, Kessler & Gentile, 1969). Gentile et al. argued that analogical reasoning was largely associative reasoning, even for adults.

A different experimental approach to the same question was taken by Willner (1964). He showed that nearly 60% of I.Q. test analogies such as *hat:head::shoe:* ? could be correctly "solved" by presentation of the C term alone. Subjects who were given the C-term "shoe" and the distractors "arm", "table", "foot", "lamp", tended to choose "foot" as the best match for "shoe". "Foot" is also the best answer to the analogy. Thus the degree of association between both the C and the D terms and the B and the C terms can affect solution choices in classical analogies (see also Grudin, 1980).

As noted earlier in this chapter, however, there is an important distinction between using associative reasoning to solve analogies because of a failure to understand relational similarity, and using associative reasoning because it gives the correct answer to the analogy (as in Willner's study). The fact that adults chose associative solutions in these studies is not evidence for a competence deficit in using relational similarity, even when the associative solutions were incorrect (after all, the adults were in the formal-operational stage of reasoning). It is important to realise that the same may be true of young children.

Most of the work testing the associative hypothesis has not recognised this distinction between competence and performance, however. For example, Achenbach (1970, 1971) suggested that a reliance on association might be a good way to distinguish children who were unable to use their full reasoning powers from those who were. To identify such children, he designed an ingenious test called the Children's Associative Responding Test, or CART. The CART consisted of 68 classical analogies, half of which had a strong associate of the C term as one of the candidate D terms (a "foil"), and half of which did not. An example of an item with a foil would be *"Pig* is to *boar* as *dog* is to ? Cat, Smoke, Rat, Turtle, *Wolf* ". The strong associate "cat" is the foil. Foils are similar to counter-suggestions, as both provide an attractive associate of the C term as an alternative possible solution to the analogy.

In order to gauge the degree of associative responding on the CART, Achenbach compared the total number of children's errors on the non-foil items to the total number of their errors on the foil items. He found that children aged from 10 to 14 years with a high number of foil errors tended to have lower I.Q.'s than other children. They also had lower grade averages in school, and lower teachers' ratings on learning effectiveness. Achenbach concluded that the CART was an important predictor of performance during the early formal-operational period of development. This conclusion was based on the assumption that children who showed an excess of foil errors on the CART were reasoning by association.

However, this may not have been the case. Once again, the question of relational difficulty arises. The fact that the children with a high number of foil errors had lower I.Q.'s could mean that they also had a poorer knowledge of the conceptual relationships underlying the analogies. This lack of knowledge could explain their poorer performance even if they were trying to reason by analogy. The finding that all of the children solved some of the foil items correctly is evidence in favour of this interpretation of Achenbach's results.

Gentile et. al. (1977) had a different criticism of Achenbach's experiment. They believed that the children who were *succeeding* on the CART were doing so by using associative strategies. Some of the correct solutions to the analogies were strong associates of the C term, and so Gentile et al. argued that associative choices could give rise to spurious evidence for an understanding of the relational similarity constraint. To test this idea, they decided to obtain associative ratings for the foil items from children. It turned out that the word clusters that were rated as most highly related were indeed those that included the correct response to the analogies. So Gentile et al.'s criticism is correct. The use of associative reasoning would give correct answers to the CART analogies, and so Achenbach's results are completely ambiguous.

As a further test of their associative hypothesis, Gentile et al. decided to see whether children's performance on the CART could be improved by training them to respond associatively. They designed three different training conditions for the foil analogies, based on the three kinds of CART responses (correct, foil and control), all involving sentence completion tasks. For example, in the *correct training* condition, 11- and 12-year-old children were asked to complete sentences like "A pig is a tame boar and a dog is a tame ? (wolf)". In the *foil training* condition, the same item would read "A pig and a boar fight like a dog and a ? (cat)", and in the *control* condition it would read "The pig and the boar and the dog smelled the ? (smoke)". Children were given feedback until they had learned the appropriate responses. Analogy performance on these 17 trained items and on the 17 untrained foil items was then compared.

Each training condition turned out to have a significant effect on the children's performance in the analogy test. All of the children chose significantly more of the trained answers in the 17 primed foil analogies than in the 17 unprimed foil analogies, irrespective of whether the answers were analogically correct or incorrect. With the untrained foil and non-foil analogies (51 in all), the children in the correct training condition chose slightly more analogically correct responses (36.9) than the children in the control training condition (33.9 correct responses), and the children in the foil training condition showed a slight depression in performance (32.8 correct responses). So training with different associations successfully led children either towards or away from the correct responses to the analogies. Gentile et al. argued that they had established that children solved analogies by associative reasoning: "... whatever else analogical reasoning is, it is in large measure an associative process" (p. 378).

However, this conclusion does not necessarily follow from their data. We do not know how the children interpreted the training that they were given. They may quite plausibly have thought that they were meant to choose the same response that they had learned during training when they were given the CART items. So Gentile et al.'s results do not provide unambiguous evidence that children use associative reasoning to solve analogies, especially as the effects of training on the unprimed analogies were very small.

In any case, as noted previously, even if we had such evidence, it would not necessarily show a deficit in competence. Children may choose associative solutions even if they understand the relational similarity constraint, just as adults do. So associative responding, like the acceptance of counter-suggestions, does not provide unambiguous evidence for the claim that younger children are unable to use the relational similarity constraint.

## Summary

Let us reconsider the three different claims made by Piaget's structural theory of analogical development in the light of the evidence discussed in this chapter.

The first claim was that the ability to reason about the relational similarity constraint was a formal-operational skill. Most of the evidence that apparently supported this claim, such as the studies by Lunzer (1965) and by Gallagher and Wright (1979), has proved difficult to interpret. The main problem with these studies was that the children may not have known the relations on which the analogies were based. Their apparent failure to demonstrate knowledge of the relational similarity constraint could thus have been due to their lack of relational knowledge.

The second claim was that reasoning about relational similarity required a special kind of higher-order reasoning, similar to that required to reason about proportional equivalence. Again, however, the evidence in support of this claim (Gallagher & Wright, 1977; Levinson & Carpenter, 1974; Lunzer, 1965) turned out to be unconvincing. Proportional reasoning does not seem to be especially related to analogy.

The third claim was that prior to the onset of formal operations, children were misled by counter-suggestions that destroyed the relational similarity constraint, and that therefore they only understood the relations in the analogies in successive terms. A related claim was that children relied on associative reasoning to solve analogies. Once more, the evidence for these claims proved to be ambiguous. Children's tendency to produce associative responses may have arisen from a lack of knowledge of the relations in the analogies (e.g. Gallagher & Wright, 1977), or from misconceptions about the task (e.g. Gentile et al., 1977).

So far, however, we do not have any direct evidence that structural theories of analogical development are wrong. In the next chapter, we turn to more recent studies that test directly each of Piaget's three claims.

CHAPTER THREE

# Testing the Claims of Structural Theory

So far we have seen that much of the evidence for a structural theory of analogical development is unconvincing. However, none of the studies that were discussed in the last chapter set out to directly challenge Piaget's claims. In this chapter, we consider recent evidence that shows clearly that the three main claims of structural theory are wrong.

## The Formal-Operational Claim:
## Analogies Based on Causal Relations

One problem that we noted with many of the experiments based on Piaget's theory was that the analogies that they used may have involved relations that were unfamiliar to the children. None of these studies included a test for relational knowledge, and so the children's failure to reason by analogy could have been due to relational difficulty. There is a clear need for a study of analogy that uses relations that are known to be understood by younger children, and that includes a control condition to check that the children possess this relational knowledge as well.

One kind of relational knowledge that very young children have is knowledge about causal relations. Research on the development of causal knowledge has demonstrated that children come to understand physical causal relations such as *cutting*, *wetting* and *melting* between the ages of 3 and 4 years (e.g. Bullock, Gelman & Baillargeon, 1982; Das

Gupta & Bryant, 1989; Schultz, 1982). The domain of physical causality thus provides a convenient means of testing Piaget's first claim.

For this test, we designed some classical analogies based on relations like cutting, melting and wetting (Goswami & Brown, 1989). Our task followed the picture analogy method devised by Piaget. However, instead of asking children to sort piles of pictures into pairs, we used a version of the multiple-choice technique. We presented the children with pictures for the A, B and C terms of each analogy, and then asked them to select a picture of the correct D term from a range of five alternatives.

The analogy task was introduced as a game about choosing pictures. A specially designed "game board" was used for the game, which had two empty spaces for pictures at one end of the board, and two at the other (see Fig. 3.1). The A and B pictures were placed together on the left-hand side of the board, and the C picture and an empty space for the D picture were on the right-hand side. The children were asked to choose a picture from among the alternative solutions to fill the empty space. They were told to select the picture that would best "finish the pattern".

The children, who were aged 3, 4 and 6 years, were required to solve eight different analogies twice during an experimental session, once on their own (*induction phase*), and then one more time with feedback (*explanation phase*). During the induction phase, the children picked a D term, but were not told whether it was correct or incorrect. During the explanation phase, they were told whether they had chosen the correct picture after each trial. If they had chosen the wrong picture on a particular trial, the correct response was indicated by the experimenter, who also explained why this was the best picture to finish the pattern. For example, in the *cutting* analogy *playdoh:cut playdoh::apple:cut apple*, the experimenter explained that on one side of the game board there was a picture of playdoh, and then a picture of playdoh that had been cut, and so on the other side of the game board the children had to pair the picture of the apple with a picture of an apple that had been cut. Feedback was specific to each trial, and was

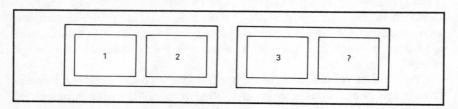

FIG. 3.1. The game board used in the Picture Analogy Task.

given regardless of whether the experimenter or the child had selected the correct response.

Four different distractors were used to test for possible alternative solution strategies. One was an associate of the C term (the associative response, e.g. a *banana* for the apple), and another was something that looked like the C term (a response based on similarity of appearance, e.g. a *round ball* for the apple). There was also a picture of the C term with a different causal transformation (e.g. a *bruised apple*) and a picture of a different object with the correct causal transformation (e.g. a *cut cake*). The fifth picture (the D term) was the correct answer to the analogy (e.g. a *cut apple*). The children were asked to describe all of the pictures, to ensure that the intended representations were clear. The pictures for the *cutting* analogy are shown in Fig. 3.2.

In addition to the analogy condition, we included a control condition to test for the children's knowledge of the relations on which the analogies were based. This condition also used a picture sequencing task, but here the four pictures were placed in an unbroken line. The child was presented with three pictures of a given causal transformation (e.g. a *cut apple*, a *cut cake*, *cut playdoh*), and was asked to find the picture of the cause of the transformation from five alternatives. The correct answer here would be a picture of a *knife*. Pictures for the control sequence in the *cutting* analogy are shown in Fig. 3.3. Successful performance in this control condition was expected to be a prerequisite for successful completion of the analogies.

This was exactly what we found. Children of all ages tested were able to solve the causal analogies, as long as they understood the causal relations on which the analogies were based. There was a strong conditional probability between knowing a relation R and solving an

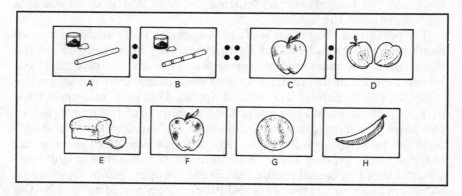

FIG. 3.2. The "Appearance Same" analogy based on "cutting" (Goswami & Brown, 1989. Reproduced with permission.).

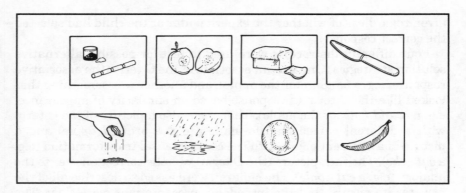

FIG. 3.3. The causal reasoning control sequence for "cutting" (Goswami & Brown, 1989. Reproduced with permission.).

analogy based on that relation. The older children (the 4- and 6-year-olds) solved more analogies than the younger children, but they also knew more of the causal relations. Performance was also better in the explanation phase than in the induction phase at all ages, as might be expected. Altogether, 52% of the 3-year-olds, 90% of the 4-year-olds and 100% of the 6-year-olds reached a criterion of 5 or more correct responses out of 8 in the explanation condition.

These performance levels are striking given the previous literature. We found that even the youngest of our subjects seemed to understand the relational similarity constraint, and could refer to it explicitly when justifying their solution choices. For example, Maria (aged 2 years, 9 months) offered the justification " 'Cause they both match, 'cause these two things are both cut" for the analogy *playdoh:cut playdoh::apple:cut apple*. As she understood the "cutting" relation, Maria could use this relation to solve the analogy.

The pattern of errors that we found suggested that the children were thinking about causal relations even when they mistakenly chose the distractors. The most frequent error was to select the picture of the correct object that had undergone the *wrong* causal transformation (for example, the picture of the bruised apple). This response could have arisen from attempts to equate the two halves of the analogies on the basis of a more general relation such as "causal transformation". Such a strategy would have led to analogies like *playdoh:cut playdoh::apple:bruised apple*. Alternatively, the children might have thought that any causal relation involving the appropriate object was a sufficient basis for a response. This latter strategy would not involve the use of relational similarity, but these two possibilities cannot be distinguished from the present data.

A different explanation of these errors is that they were based on perceptual similarity. The objects that had undergone the incorrect causal transformation shared a high degree of perceptual similarity with the C term, and so the children could have been erroneously selecting responses on the basis of this similarity (Gentner, Ratterman & Campbell, in prep.). For example, in the *cutting* analogy, the children might simply have reasoned that they needed another picture of an apple, and so they might have picked the picture of the *bruised apple* rather than the picture of the *cut apple*. Although this alternative explanation can only be partially correct (it predicts that the children should have chosen the *cut apple* and the *bruised apple* equally frequently, which they did not do), a second experiment was carried out to ensure that perceptual similarity was not also supporting *correct* analogical reasoning.

In this second experiment, the appearance of the objects depicted in the analogies was changed by the causal transformation, so that they no longer shared as much perceptual similarity with the A and the C terms. For example, for the *cutting* analogy, the pictures were: (A) a *loaf of bread*, (B) a *slice of bread*, (C) a *lemon* and (D) a *slice of lemon*. To test the perceptual similarity hypothesis, an exact perceptual match for the C term was added to the distractors. For example, in the *cutting* analogy, a lemon that was identical to the picture used for the C term was included. A second group of 3-, 4- and 6-year-olds was asked to solve both these new (Appearance Differs) analogies and the previous (Appearance Same) analogies. The stimuli for the *cutting* analogy in the Appearance Differs condition are shown in Fig. 3.4.

If correct responding in Experiment 1 was partially based on perceptual similarity, then the children should have performed more

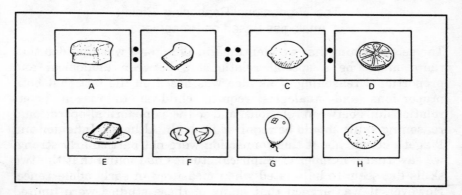

FIG. 3.4. The "Appearance Differs" analogy based on "cutting" (Goswami & Brown, 1989. Reproduced with permission.).

poorly with the Appearance Differs analogies than with the Appearance Same analogies. No such difference in performance was found. Overall, 81% of the 4-year-olds and 100% of the 6-year-olds reached criterion with the perceptually dissimilar Appearance Differs analogies, compared to 93% and 95% respectively with the Appearance Same analogies. Although the 3-year-olds performed more poorly with the Appearance Differs analogies than with the Appearance Same analogies (29% correct compared to 48% correct respectively), the difference in performance was not statistically significant. So correct responding in Experiment 1 was unlikely to have been due to choosing pictures on the basis of perceptual similarity.

The errors that the children made were also analysed. Again, it was found that the most popular distractor was the picture of the incorrect causal transformation, implying a focus on causal relations. As the children hardly ever chose the identity match, the idea that this error was based on perceptual similarity seems to be wrong.

Most importantly of all with respect to the relational difficulty hypothesis, however, this second experiment also found a strong conditional relationship between performance in the control condition that measured relational knowledge (which was altered to correspond to the Appearance Differs analogies) and the children's ability to solve the causal analogies. These results provide genuine support for the relational difficulty hypothesis. When children have the relevant relational knowledge, then they can solve analogies long before they reach the formal-operational period. So even 3-year-old children can reason by analogy in the classical A:B::C:D task, as long as they understand the relations used in the analogies.

### The "Proportional Reasoning" Claim:
### Analogies Based on Proportions

The second claim that we identified in Chapter 2 was the idea that there might be a special relationship between analogical and proportional reasoning. This idea was based on the fact that both proportions and analogies require children to reason about relationships between relations, and so the same formal-operational reasoning skills should be required for both. Although Inhelder and Piaget's claims about this connection were not particularly strong, we saw that a number of empirical studies had found that the two skills did seem to be related when measured in early adolescence. However, it was argued that many of these studies were limited because they used a test of proportional reasoning that essentially required children to articulate the relational similarity constraint.

An alternative approach would be to test the proposed relationship between proportional reasoning and analogical reasoning directly, by designing an analogy task based on proportions.

In an early version of the picture sequencing task used in the Goswami and Brown (1989) study, I attempted to devise such a task (Goswami, 1989). The stimuli were pictures of proportions, and the children were told that they were going to play a game about matching patterns. The proportions were 1/4, 1/2, 3/4 and whole, and the stimuli were pictures of different shapes (circle, square, rectangle, triangle and diamond). The relevant proportion of each stimulus was shaded in yellow. An example of a proportional analogy would be *half circle:half rectangle::quarter circle:quarter rectangle*. To solve the analogy correctly, the child has to reason about the equality of proportions. This analogy is depicted in Fig. 3.5.

Four distractors were used in this analogy task. These were (1) a picture of the correct shape with the wrong proportion shaded (e.g. 3/4 rectangle), (2) a picture of the wrong shape with the correct proportion shaded (e.g. 1/4 square), (3) another picture of the B term and (4) another picture of the C term. The fifth possible choice was the correct answer. The distractors were intended to pick up responses that were either based on a partial extraction of the relevant relations (e.g. concentrating on either shape [response 1] or proportion [response 2]), or on some kind

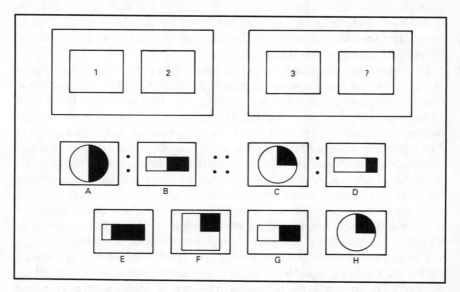

FIG. 3.5. An example of a proportional analogy (reproduced with permission from Goswami, 1989).

of similarity matching or perseveration (e.g. matching to the B term or to the C term).

To measure understanding of the relation of proportional equivalence across changes in shape, a control condition was included in the experiment. Here the children were required to complete sequences of four pictures of the same proportion (e.g. 1/4 circle, 1/4 rectangle, 1/4 square, 1/4 diamond). To complete the sequences correctly, the children had to match the shapes on the basis of proportional equivalence, but without having to reason about this relation analogically.

As in the causal relations studies, it was expected that children's analogical performance would be related to their relational knowledge, and this was exactly what was found. Children aged 4, 6 and 7 years took part in the experiment, and the two older groups performed extremely well in the proportional equivalence control condition, scoring 88% and 91% correct respectively. They were also very successful at solving the proportional analogies, completing 79% (6 years) and 87% (7 years) of them correctly. The 4-year-olds performed much more poorly in the control condition, correctly equating proportions in only 56% of the sequences, and they were also less successful at solving the analogies, completing only 31% correctly. However, as in the Goswami and Brown (1989) study, there was a relationship between analogical success and relational understanding: 75% of the children who succeeded in solving a significant number of analogies were those who had also performed well in the control task. So once again, if children understand the relations on which an analogy is based, then they can usually solve that analogy. This is just as the relational difficulty hypothesis would predict.

The most important finding in this study, however, was that children as young as 4 years of age could reason analogically about proportions. This finding is important for two reasons. The first is that it shows that some understanding of proportional equivalence is present at a much younger age than Piaget (and also Lunzer) would predict. The second is that it directly contradicts the version of Piaget's theory that places the emergence of both analogical and proportional reasoning in the formal-operational period. Although we cannot decide from this experiment whether reasoning about the relational similarity constraint and reasoning about proportional equivalence require the same cognitive skills, we can say that analogical reasoning, and at least some forms of proportional reasoning, are present quite early in development.

The type of proportional reasoning involved in these analogies may not be the kind of proportional reasoning that Piaget was interested in, however. The proportional relations in Goswami (1989) were perceptual rather than logical, and this may be very important. A perceptual understanding of proportions may differ from a logical understanding.

Although 1/4 circle and 1/4 rectangle do not look similar in shape, there is some perceptual similarity between them, and so while finding the correct solution to the proportional analogies does require a logical understanding of relational similarity, it may not require a logical understanding of proportional equivalence.

There is at least one other piece of evidence that very young children can understand proportional equivalence when the task is a perceptual one. Spinillo and Bryant (1991) asked 4-, 5-, 6- and 7-year-olds to make proportional equivalence judgements that involved deciding which one of two boxes of coloured bricks matched the proportion represented in a picture. For example, if the picture (which was quite small) was coloured 5/8 blue and 3/8 white, then the children were asked to make a choice between a box containing 5/8 blue and 3/8 white bricks (the correct choice), and another box containing 3/8 blue and 5/8 white bricks. Sometimes the proportions in the picture and in the boxes of bricks were in the same alignment (e.g. horizontal division of the blue and white proportions: the *perceptual similarity* condition), and sometimes they differed (e.g. picture = horizontal division of blue and white sections, bricks = vertical division: the *perceptual dissimilarity* condition). This experiment also involved the recognition of relational similarity. The task used by Spinillo and Bryant is shown in Fig. 3.6.

Spinillo and Bryant found that the older children (the 6- and 7-year-olds) succeeded in making proportional equivalence judgements in both the perceptual similarity condition (same alignment of picture and bricks) and the perceptual dissimilarity condition (different alignment of picture and bricks). They could also recognise proportional equivalence when two pictures of different sizes were used to represent the proportion in one box of bricks, and when the alignment of the pictures and of the bricks in the box differed. So the children could make proportional judgements even when perceptual matching across changes in size was impossible. It should be noted that in order to do so, they had to recognise similarities in the *relationships* between the amount of blue and white in the pictures and in the boxes. So the children had to respond on the basis of relational similarity.

Spinillo and Bryant have an interesting explanation for their positive result. It is that the children were actually making proportional judgements on the basis of "part–part" relations. For example, the children could match the picture to the correct box of bricks by recognising that there was a greater proportion of blue than of white in both the picture and in the box of bricks *without* knowing what that proportion actually was. Use of the part–part relation "greater than" (as in "there are more blue bricks than white bricks") would not necessarily require an understanding of proportional equivalence.

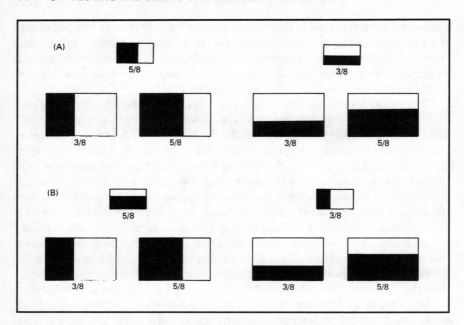

FIG. 3.6. The two conditions in Spinillo and Bryant's (1991) task. (A) Perceptual similarity condition; (B) perceptual dissimilarity condition. Reproduced with permission.

However, the use of part–part relations would still require an understanding of relational similarity. The children would still have to decide whether the relation "greater than" applied *in the same way* to the proportions of blue and white in the bricks and in the picture. This raises the possibility that the proportional analogies might also have been solved on a part–part basis. In the Proportional Analogy task, the correct solution could have been selected on the basis of reasoning that, for example, a rectangle with a little bit of yellow (1/4) was matched by a circle with a little bit of yellow (1/4). Some of the children in the study did spontaneously make remarks along these lines. However, whether they were succeeding in the task by using part–part relations or by using proportional equivalence, the children must still have been using the relational similarity constraint. This is because the distractors included more than one example of the correct proportion (e.g. 1/4).

The idea that proportional reasoning is linked to analogical reasoning thus requires a more specific definition of which kind of proportional reasoning is involved. If a perceptual understanding of proportions is sufficient for analogy, such as the use of part–part relations, then the two kinds of reasoning may be related. If Piaget was talking about a logical understanding of proportions (which seems more likely), then this kind of proportional reasoning does not seem to be directly involved in the development of reasoning by analogy. Children can use the relational similarity constraint long before they seem able to reason logically about proportional equivalence.

## The Successive Reasoning Claim:
## Evidence from Thematic Analogies

Let us turn to Piaget's third claim, which was that younger children understand the relations in an analogy in a successive way. His interpretation of their willingness to accept false counter-suggestions as adequate analogical solutions was that they did not understand that there was a constraint on how the relations in the analogy were connected. A related claim put forward by other authors was that younger children may use associative reasoning rather than relational similarity to solve analogies, selecting answers that are strong associates of the C term rather than the answers that are specified by the relational similarity constraint.

How can the successive/associative claim be tested? We saw in Chapter 2 that some authors have tried to use a multiple-choice technique as such a test, by including counter-suggestions among the distractors in multiple-choice items. However, in many of these experiments, it proved impossible to distinguish between solutions based on analogical reasoning and solutions based on associative reasoning (e.g. Achenbach, 1971). A methodology that explicitly tests the successive notion and that also distinguishes between associative and analogical solutions is needed.

In an effort to devise such a method, we (Goswami & Brown, 1990) adapted the picture analogy technique to enable us to contrast solutions based on familiar associative relations with solutions based on relational similarity. The associative distractors that we used were thematic relations (such as *fish–net* or *dog–bone*), relations that are known to be highly attractive to young children. There is ample evidence that in category sorting tasks, 3-, 4- and 5-year-olds will sort pictures on the basis of thematic relations rather than category relations, pairing *dogs* with *bones* rather than with other animals, or *fish* with *nets* rather than with other fish (depending on the verbal instructions given; e.g. Bauer & Mandler, 1989; Markman & Hutchinson, 1984; Nelson, 1977; Smiley & Brown, 1979). For the young child, thematic relations seem to provide a natural way of relating objects in the world.

In fact, many of Piaget's counter-suggestions were thematically related to the C term in his analogies (e.g. *bicycle–pump, ship–siren*). So the use of thematic distractors in the multiple-choice task should provide a very strong test of younger children's understanding of the relations in analogies. If they choose thematic responses without taking into account the relation between the A and the B terms in the analogy, then this would imply that they understand the relations in analogies in a successive way. However, if they can override the attraction of familiar thematic relations and choose the analogy responses, then this would imply an understanding of the relational similarity constraint.

In our thematic analogies, the *wrong* response to the analogy was a thematic relation, and the *correct* response was a less frequent associate of the C term. For example, in the analogy *bird:nest::dog:dog house/bone*, the picture of the *dog house* was the correct (Analogy) response, while the picture of the *bone* was the familiar thematic relation (Thematic response). The other distractors that we used in the experiment were a perceptual similarity match (e.g. another *dog*) and a category match (a distractor commonly used in category sorting tasks, e.g. a *cat*). We devised 10 different thematic analogies, all based on simple relations such as "lives in". An example of a thematic analogy is shown in Fig. 3.7.

Children aged 4, 5 and 9 years took part in the experiment. As a further test of their ability to use the relational similarity constraint, we included a prediction task. The children were asked to predict the solution to the analogies before they saw the picture distractors. This was intended as a test of mental reasoning, as one of Piaget's criteria for full analogical understanding was the ability to operate mentally on relations.

Finally, a control condition was devised to check that the Analogy response was not simply the preferred match for the C term. In this control condition, the C term was presented alone, and the children were

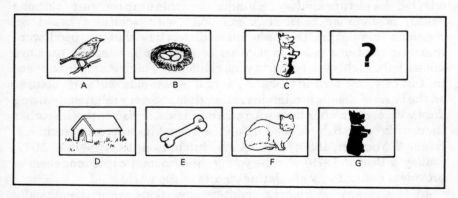

FIG. 3.7. The "Lives In" analogy after the Thematic Analogies Task (reproduced with permission from Goswami & Brown, 1990).

given the four possible solution pictures. They were then asked to decide which picture "went best" with the C term. Their choices in the control condition provided a measure of their preference for the Analogy response in the absence of the A:B pair. As a further check of children's understanding of the relational similarity constraint, we also asked them to tell us whether there could be another correct answer in both the control condition (where there could) and in the analogy condition (where there could not).

We predicted that if the children could solve the analogies by using the relational similarity constraint, then they should choose the Analogy response significantly more frequently in the analogy condition than in the control condition. This was indeed what we found. The Analogy response was chosen 94% of the time by the 9-year-olds, 66% of the time by the 5-year-olds and 59% of the time by the 4-year-olds in the analogy condition when this was received first. The corresponding figures for the control condition were 39% (9-year-olds), 32% (5-year-olds) and 32% (4-year-olds), respectively. So the children were able to successfully resist the Thematic distractor as a solution to the analogies, and to select the responses specified by the relational similarity constraint.

They were also frequently able to predict the correct solution to the analogies before being shown the different distractors. The percentage of correct predictions was 87% for the 9-year-olds, 54% for the 5-year-olds and 35% for the 4-year-olds. The poor performance of the youngest children was due to a verbal tendency to produce thematic associates of the C term. Altogether, 66% (4-year-olds) and 72% (5-year-olds) of the erroneous predictions were of this type. Once the children saw the relevant pictures, however, they went on to solve many of the analogies correctly. This is an important finding, as many of the experiments supporting the associative hypothesis used verbal questioning techniques (see Chapter 2). With the picture task, even the youngest subjects could resist associative responses, and they could also use the relational similarity constraint to work out mental solutions to some of the analogies.

A charming example of this comes from Lucas, aged 4 years and 7 months, who was asked to predict the solution to the pictorial analogy *bird:nest::dog: ?.* He reasoned as follows: "Bird lays eggs in her nest [some eggs were actually shown in the nest in the picture]. Dog...dogs lay babies, and the babies are ... umm ... and the name of the babies is puppy!" The experimenter suggested that they take a look at the pictures. Lucas protested "I don't have to look. And the name of the baby is puppy!" However, once Lucas did look at the different pictures (a *bone*, a *dog*, a *cat* and a *dog house*), he immediately selected the picture of the *dog house* to complete the analogy (Goswami & Brown, 1990).

Lucas seems to have first solved the analogy by using a different relation ("type of offspring") to that chosen by the experimenters ("lives in"). However, when he saw that a picture of a puppy did not appear among the possible completion terms (although they did include a picture of a dog), he changed the relation on which his response was based. Both of Lucas' answers show use of the relational similarity constraint, and they also provide evidence of truly *mental* operations: Lucas was able to reason by analogy prior to seeing the solution options, and then to change his response in accordance with the relational similarity constraint.

Finally, whereas the majority of the children in our experiment agreed that there could be another right answer in the control condition, they did not permit an equivalent flexibility in the analogy condition. Most of the children (75%) maintained that there could be only one correct answer in the analogy condition (i.e. the Analogy response). This is further evidence for an understanding of the relational similarity constraint. If the 4-year-olds had had a successive understanding of the relations in the analogies, then they would have allowed more than one right answer in the analogy condition as well as in the control condition. Thus all of Piaget's criteria for true analogical reasoning can be met by children as young as 4 years of age. Analogical reasoning is not a formal-operational skill after all.

## Summary

The research reviewed here has shown quite comprehensively that structural theories of analogical development were based on misleading data. Most of these data came from experiments that asked young children to reason about relations that were too difficult for them. When this impediment was removed, then children as young as 3 and 4 years of age could reason by analogy in the classical task. They could also ignore counter-suggestions that destroyed the analogies, they showed a flexible understanding of the relational similarity constraint, and they could mentally predict the solutions to the analogies. They were even able to reason analogically about perceptual proportions. The different claims made by structural theory have been fully tested. There are no longer any grounds for maintaining that there is an age-based shift in the ability to reason about relational similarity.

CHAPTER FOUR

# Information-processing Accounts of Classical Analogical Reasoning

A rather different approach to studying the development of analogical reasoning is provided by the information-processing framework. The information-processing approach is concerned with *how* analogical reasoning occurs. Its aim is to specify the different basic information processes that are used in reasoning by analogy, and to establish how these different processes are combined when analogies are solved. Sternberg's was probably the first information-processing model of the components of analogical reasoning, and it has been very influential in cognitive psychology (Sternberg, 1977). However, when considering information-processing models, it is important to remember that the components are only postulated processes. Although intended as primitive and basic information processes that are used in analogical reasoning, they do not *necessarily* correspond to independent mental operations.

Information-processing models of analogical reasoning were not originally developmental models, but we will consider them here because cognitive psychologists have used them to ask developmental questions. The main questions are whether the different components are combined differently by adults and by children, or are combined differently by children of different ages. Furthermore, some of the information-processing components correspond to either measures of relational knowledge, or to measures of knowledge of the relational similarity constraint. These components are directly relevant to our hypothesis about the differing roles of these factors in the development of analogical reasoning, and it is these specific aspects of information-processing research that will be considered in this chapter.

## STERNBERG'S COMPONENTIAL MODEL OF ANALOGICAL REASONING

### The Components

Sternberg's information-processing model of analogical reasoning was based on a consideration of how subjects might generate solutions to forced-choice analogies of the form A:B::C: D1, D2. He subdivided this generation process into six independent informational steps, or six postulated components. The first of these was *encoding*. During encoding, the subject had to perceive each term in the analogy, and then had to access the attributes relevant to the terms in semantic memory. The second component was *inference*. Here the subject had to discover the relation between the A and the B terms, and to store this relation in working memory. The third component was *mapping*, whereby the subject discovered the relation between the A and the C terms in the analogy. The mapping step was meant to be the point at which the first half of the analogy was linked to the second. Following mapping came the *application* component. During application, the subject had to apply a relation analogous to the relation inferred at step 2 (inference) from the C term to each answer option (D1, D2). The fifth step was *justification*: Sternberg argued that in some analogies the relation between the C and the D terms might not correspond exactly to the relation inferred between the A and the B terms, and that in these circumstances the subject would need to justify one of the presented answer options as superior to the others. Finally, the subjects had to *respond* with the answer of their choice. An example of how these components were thought to be used to solve the analogy *Washington:1::Lincoln: 10, 5* is given in Table 4.1.

It is worth noting in passing that the *mapping* component does not represent a necessary step in solving analogies. To work out that the correct solution to the analogy in Table 4.1 is "5", the subject does not need to figure out a relationship between Washington and Lincoln. He or she can simply work out that the A–B relation is "portrait on currency", and then apply this relation to the C term. There is no need to relate A and C. In fact, Sternberg himself later decided that this component of analogical reasoning was optional (e.g. Sternberg & Rifkin, 1979).

TABLE 4.1
The Componential Steps in Solving the Analogy
Washington:1::Lincoln:5[a]

| Process | Analogy Term or Relation | Relevant Attributes and Values |
|---|---|---|
| Encoding | Washington | [(president (first)), (portrait on currency (dollar)). (war hero (Revolutionary))] |
|  | 1 | [(counting number (one)), (ordinal position (first)), (amount (one unit))] |
|  | Lincoln | [(president (sixteenth)), (portrait on currency (five dollars)), (war hero (Civil))] |
|  | 10 | [(counting number (ten)), (ordinal position (tenth)), (amount (ten units))] |
|  | 5 | [(counting number (five)), (ordinal position (fifth)), (amount (five units))] |
| Inference | Washington → 1 | [(president (ordinal position (first))), (portrait on currency (amount (dollar))), (Ø)] |
| Mapping | Washington → Lincoln | [(presidents (first, sixteenth)), (portraits on currency (dollar, five dollars)), (war heroes (Revolutionary, Civil))] |
| Application | Lincoln → 10 | [(Ø), (Ø), (Ø)] |
|  | Lincoln → 5 | [(Ø), (portrait on currency (amount (five dollars))), (Ø)] |

[a]Sternberg (1977). Copyright 1977 by the American Psychological Association. Reprinted with permission.

With respect to the relational difficulty hypothesis, the important components of the model are *inference* and *application*. The inference component provides a measure of children's ability to work out the relation between the A and the B terms in the analogy. The application component provides a measure of children's ability to work out a relation between the C and the D terms that is analogous to this A–B relation. Unfortunately, however, we cannot simply equate inference with relational knowledge and application with the relational similarity constraint, as there is also the child's knowledge of the relationship between the C and the D terms to consider. In order to apply the relational similarity constraint, children must also know this latter relation. So both of these components are measures of relational knowledge, and application is also a measure of children's understanding of the relational similarity constraint.

## The Task

To find out whether children could use the six different components of analogical reasoning, and whether the availability of these components varied with age, Sternberg designed two classical analogy tasks based on schematic pictures of human figures (Sternberg & Rifkin, 1979). The child's job was to select the correct completion term for each analogy from two alternatives. In one task, the figures differed in terms of "separable" attributes that could be varied independently, such as hats and suits. Four kinds of attribute were varied in these analogies: hat colour (black or white), suit pattern (striped or spotted), hand gear (umbrella or briefcase) and footwear (shoes or boots). In the other task, the figures differed in terms of "integral" attributes: in order to depict any one attribute, it was necessary to depict the others. These were called "People Piece" analogies. The "People Piece" figures varied in height (tall, short), garment colour (black, white), sex (female, male) and weight (thin, fat). Examples of the two kinds of analogy are shown in Fig. 4.1.

Sternberg and Rifkin thought that the ability to reason about integral attributes might differ developmentally from the ability to reason about separable attributes. They therefore presented the integral and the separable analogies to groups of children aged 8, 10 and 12 years, and to 19-year-old college students. The children were told about the attributes making up the analogies (hats, height, etc.), and their instructions were to solve the problems by choosing the D term that was "the same as and different from the third picture in the same ways that the second picture is the same as and different from the first picture"

FIG. 4.1. The schematic analogies used by Sternberg and Rifkin (1979). Reproduced with permission.

(p. 207). So the importance of using the relational similarity constraint was made quite explicit.

The analogies were presented in small booklets, each of which contained 16 analogies. A maximum solution time of 64 sec. per booklet was permitted, which must have created quite a time pressure for the younger subjects. Sternberg and Rifkin found that the 8-year-olds were at chance on the analogy task. They solved 42% of the schematic analogies and 48% of the People Piece analogies correctly (chance responding would be 50%). The 10-year-olds' performance was significantly better: they solved 63% of each kind of analogy correctly. The 12-year-olds and the college students performed at roughly comparable levels, solving 76% and 72% of the schematic analogies and 72% and 83% of the People Piece analogies respectively.

To determine whether the different component processes contributed differently to children's solutions as age increased, Sternberg and Rifkin estimated the amount of time that each age group spent in executing the different component processes as the number of attributes that changed from A to B, A to C, and C to $D_{true}$ was varied. For example, in the separable analogy in Fig. 4.1, the number of attributes that change from A to B is 1 (hat colour). The number of attributes that change from A to C is 3 (suit pattern, hand gear and footwear). So in this analogy, the execution of the inference component should take less time than the execution of the mapping component. By systematically varying the number of attributes that change per component, and then comparing solution times, Sternberg and Rifkin could estimate the components used by children of different ages. From their analyses, they concluded that all the age groups used the inference, encoding, application and response components, but that the younger children (8-year-olds) did not use the mapping component. The older children were also faster at executing the different components, which is not surprising. This can be seen in the graphs reproduced in Fig. 4.2.

Sternberg and Rifkin concluded that they had shown a developmental change in analogy solution:

> The use of mapping requires recognition of a higher-order relation between two relations: that which relates the A and B terms to the C and D terms. Previous research (Inhelder & Piaget, 1958) has suggested the relatively late development of higher-order similarity relations and their considerable complexity relative to other kinds of relations (Beth & Piaget, 1966). Ability to perceive such relationships appears to form in stages. Thus, it is quite possible that children as young as second grade [8-year-olds] may recognise the lower-order similarity that relates terms A and B and terms C and D, but may have difficulty recognising the

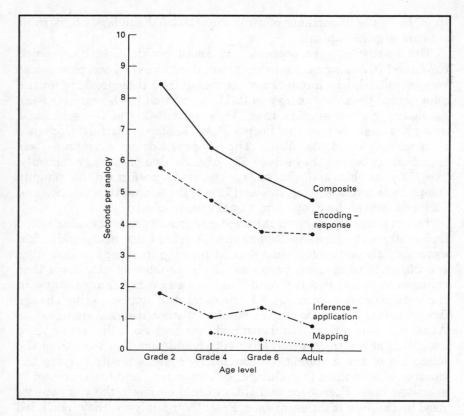

FIG. 4.2. Use of the components at different ages in the People Piece Task (reproduced with permission from Sternberg & Rifkin, 1979).

higher-order similarity relating the lower-order one ... younger children may not yet be attuned to the complex similarity relationship required in mapping between two relations (p. 226).

In view of the optional nature of the mapping component, this conclusion is surprising. As I argued earlier, it is the *application* component that seems to correspond most closely to a measure of children's knowledge of the relational similarity constraint. The mapping component does not measure higher-order similarity, and is not even necessary for successful analogical reasoning. So a failure to use mapping cannot be equated with an inability to reason about relational similarity. Sternberg and Rifkin seem to have reached a similar conclusion to that of structural theorists about analogical development, but for surprising reasons.

## Associative Reasoning in Componential Tasks

Interestingly, Sternberg and his group also came up with a familiar explanation of how the younger children were solving the analogies. They proposed that the children were reasoning by association. To investigate this possibility further, Sternberg designed a different analogical reasoning task based on verbal classical analogies (Sternberg & Nigro, 1980). This task was intended to measure the role of associative reasoning in children's analogical solutions.

In this task, children aged from 9 to 15 years and college students were given three kinds of verbal analogy to solve. The analogy problems varied in the number of terms that made up the stem of the analogy, so that the simplest type of problem had the conventional three terms (A:B::C: D1, D2, D3, D4), while the most complex type of problem had only one term (A: B1::C1:D1; B2::C2:D2; B3::C3:D3; B4::C4:D4). The aim was to vary the amount of information-processing time required to solve each type of analogy. For example, whereas 7 items need to be encoded in the three-term-stem analogies, 13 need to be encoded in the one-term-stem analogies, and so the amount of time needed to execute the encoding component should be longer in the latter. Examples of each kind of problem would be:

1. *Three-term stem*: *Narrow:wide::question:* trial, statement, *answer*, ask;
2. *Two-term stem*: *Win:lose::* dislike:hate, ear:hear, enjoy:like, *above: below*;
3. *One-term stem*: *Weak:* sick::circle:shape, *strong::poor:rich*, small::garden:grow, health::solid:firm.

It can be seen that the degree of the semantic association between the last term in the stem of the analogy and the first term in the correct answer option varies in each case. For example, the degree of association between "question" and "answer" in the three-term-stem analogy is greater than the degree of association between "lose" and "above" in the two-term-stem analogy. Degree of association was manipulated intentionally across the different problem types, so that the role of associative reasoning in analogical responding could be estimated.

The examples given above are all based on the relationship of "opposite". Overall, five different relations were used in the analogies, namely antonymy (e.g. *start:finish::far:near*), synonymy (e.g. *under: beneath::pain:hurt*), functional relations (e.g. *shoes:feet::hat:head*), linear ordering (e.g. *yesterday:today::before:now*) and category membership (e.g. *noon:time::west:direction*). However, the experimenters did not measure the children's understanding of these different relations, which clearly vary in difficulty.

To measure developmental differences in analogical reasoning, the different number of executions of the different components for each analogy type (plus association ratings) were used as the independent variables in a series of multiple-regression equations, the dependent variables being response time and error rate. These analyses showed that there was a developmental difference in the pattern of both response times and error rates as the type of analogy problem varied. The younger children's response times and error rates were correlated with the degree of association between the last term in the stem and the first term in the answer option of the analogies. Furthermore, they did not show any effects of information-processing complexity. They were as fast at solving the analogies that required more information-processing steps or inferences (one-term stem) as the analogies that required fewer inferences (three-term stem). This would not be predicted by a componential model of reasoning, as the former should take longer to solve than the latter.

In contrast, the response times and error rates of the 15-year-olds and of the college students *were* correlated with inference difficulty, and were not correlated with the associative strength of the C–D relationship. The older subjects also took longer to solve the one-term-stem analogies (many inferences) than to solve the three-term-stem analogies (fewer inferences), and showed no effects of association. So the performance of the older children seemed to depend on relational difficulty, whereas that of the younger children depended on associative strength.

Sternberg and Nigro concluded that they had found further evidence for a developmental difference between the younger (9- to 12-year-olds) and older subjects when it came to reasoning by analogy:

> The fact that these [younger] children do not increase the amount of time spent on inference as a function of the number of inferences potentially to be made suggests that association is used, at least to some extent, as a substitute for full reasoning by analogy. Older children appear to rely almost exclusively on reasoning processes in analogy solution: High association does not facilitate solution. Moreover, increases in the number of inferences to be made result in an increase in response latency, as would be required in any model based exclusively upon reasoning processes (p. 34).

So once again, it is only older children who are credited with complete analogical reasoning. This conclusion was accepted by most information-processing theorists. Sternberg and Nigro were not alone in their field in believing that associative reasoning played an important role in younger children's performance in classical analogy tasks, as we will see later in this chapter (e.g. Goldman, Pellegrino, Parseghian & Sallis, 1982; Goldman & Pellegrino, 1984). However, the associative evidence largely depended on experiments that did not control for relational difficulty (see Goswami, 1991a, for a fuller discussion), and we will not refute the hypothesis again here. As we saw in Chapter 3, younger children are quite capable of distinguishing between analogical and associative solutions when relational knowledge is controlled.

Let us focus instead on the new view of analogy that is offered by the information-processing account, namely the postulation of separable measurable components in analogical reasoning. More recent studies have tried to examine children's ability to use these different components in more detail. We will concentrate in particular on evidence for children's use of the inference and the application components, as these are most relevant to our interest in the separate factors of relational knowledge and knowledge of the relational similarity constraint.

## CHILDREN'S ABILITY TO USE THE COMPONENT PROCESSES

Perhaps the most important of these two components for our purposes is the inference component. Children's use of inference in information-processing tasks enables us to test the prediction that their analogical performance should be related to relational difficulty. Children who fail to execute the inference component successfully are failing to identify the relation linking the A term to the B term, and so according to the relational difficulty hypothesis they should be unlikely to go on to solve the analogy. On the other hand, children who are successful at the inference stage should solve the analogy successfully as long as they know the corresponding relation for the C term, and can use the relational similarity constraint (unless other factors intervene).

The second component that is important for the relational difficulty hypothesis is application. Our knowledge-based view of analogical reasoning asserts that children can recognise relational similarity from very early in development. So if a child can use the inference component successfully, then that child should also be able to use the application component, as this involves relational similarity. Unfortunately, however, as noted earlier, the application component does not provide a pure measure of the relational similarity constraint, as relational knowledge is also involved in application. In order to equate the relations between the A and the B terms and the C and the D terms, the child must also know the relevant relation that links C and D. So the successful solution of classical analogies requires the appropriate use of *both* inference and application.

## Measuring Inference and Application

Authors using the information-processing framework to investigate the development of analogical reasoning have also been aware of the importance of the inference component. For example, Goldman et al. (1982) argued that inference might be one of the component processes that contributed most to developmental and individual differences in analogy performance. They also proposed two other possible sources of developmental and individual differences in analogical reasoning: the accuracy with which children could recognise the correct responses in analogy tasks, and the ease with which they were distracted by incorrect solutions. These latter factors involve an understanding of relational similarity as well as the possession of the relevant relational knowledge. To recognise correct responses and to ignore incorrect responses, children must know the relation between C and D that corresponds to that inferred between A and B, and must also understand the importance of the relational similarity constraint. Goldman et al. decided to use an information-processing analysis to try to isolate these different sources of developmental and individual differences.

In their experiment, they asked 8- and 10-year-old children to solve classical analogies such as *"Dog is to Bark as Cat is to ?"*, presented in a written format. During the solution of each analogy, the children were "walked through" the different components in the componential model, so that each one could be measured separately. First, they were shown the A and the B terms of the analogy, and were asked to explain how they "went together". This constituted the measure of *inference*. Next, they were shown the first three terms in the stem of the analogy (A:B::C), and were asked to produce a D term by thinking of a word that went with the C term in the same way that the A and the B terms went together. This explicit instruction to use the relational similarity constraint provided a measure of *application*. The children were then shown five possible completion terms for the analogy (A:B::C: D1, D2, D3, D4, D5), and were asked to select one of these responses. The probability of recognising the correct forced-choice response given incorrect generation of the analogical relation at the inference step was taken as a measure of *response recognition* (presumably the failure to find an appropriate match for the incorrect A:B relation led children to change their inference, as we saw with Lucas' *dog:puppy* inference in Chapter 3). Finally, the probability of selecting an incorrect forced-choice response given correct inference and application on the generation task was taken as a measure of *distractor interference*.

Goldman et al. argued that the application, response recognition and distractor interference measures all involved the processing of relations from more than a single pair of terms. According to this definition, these components should all measure the relational similarity constraint. However, this is only true of the application and the response recognition components. The distractor interference component is different. This measure was designed to gauge the children's susceptibility to associative responding, as some of the distractors were strong associates of the C terms. While children who are misled into choosing the wrong response to the analogy after generating the correct relation between A and B may be processing both pairs of relations, they are not comparing them for relational similarity. Nevertheless, Goldman et al. decided to use regression analyses to see how well these different factors predicted successful performance in their forced-choice analogy test after controlling for age.

They found that the application, recognition and distraction components were the measures that were most strongly related to the children's performance with the analogies. This is an interesting result. Goldman et al. interpreted it to mean that the primary cause of developmental differences in analogical reasoning was the ability to co-ordinate and compare sets of relations (i.e. to use the relational similarity constraint). Emphasising the role of distractor interference (the associative measure), they argued that younger children had "a weaker understanding of the inherent nature of analogy and the constraints on this inductive reasoning task" ... "the present research ... strongly indicate[s] some type of simpler associative understanding of analogy" ... "different models of analogy solution are necessary to characterize the development of analogical reasoning" (pp. 557–558).

However, a by-now-familiar objection can be made to this conclusion, and it concerns relational difficulty. The importance of the response recognition component suggests that the younger children may have had relational knowledge that was inadequate for solving many of the analogies. While the older children could recognise the correct relationship from the distractors even when they could not generate it for themselves, the younger children could not, perhaps because they did not know these relations in the first place. In fact, Goldman et al. also found that the inference component was a significant predictor of analogical success, as the relational difficulty hypothesis would predict.

## The Extraction and Combination of Relations
## in Geometric Analogies

Information-processing theorists have also studied children's understanding of the relational similarity constraint by examining their ability to extract and combine relations in geometric analogies. Geometric forms provide a rather different measure of relational knowledge, because they usually have no intrinsic relational meaning. The child's job in a geometric analogy is simply to extract the relevant geometric attributes, and then to combine them into the relation constituting the analogy. For example, in the geometric analogy *large red circle:small blue circle::large red square:?*, the child who answers correctly must work out that the relevant colour is blue, the relevant size is small, and the relevant shape is a square. The correct answer to the analogy is thus a *small blue square*. Geometric analogies also provide another way of manipulating the information-processing load of the task. As the number of attributes and transformations that the children have to consider in order to generate a successful solution is varied, their ability to solve the geometric analogies might vary as well.

A good example of the geometric approach comes from a paper by Bisanz, Bisanz and Lefevre (1984), who varied the attribute structure of their stimuli by creating what they called "dot analogies". These dot analogies were based on transformations of number. The A:B part of the analogy was made up of two sets of dots that varied in attributes that Bisanz et al. defined as *magnitude* and *direction*. For example, the A term might have 3 dots and the B term 5 dots, giving a magnitude of (2) and a direction of (+). The C term in this analogy might then have 4 dots, in which case the correct D term needed to have 6 dots (the relation required to solve the analogy being "+2"). The distractors either had 8 dots (correct in terms of direction but not of magnitude) or 2 dots (correct in terms of magnitude but not of direction). This example of a dot analogy is shown in Fig. 4.3.

Bisanz et al. designed these problem triples in order to enable them to distinguish between different possible solution strategies. They reasoned that subjects who attended to the attribute of *direction* only would consider both responses (a) and (b) in Fig. 4.3 to be correct. Subjects who attended to the attribute of *magnitude* only would consider both responses (a) and (c) to be correct. Both of these solutions are of course incorrect, as they are based on only partial extraction of the appropriate relation. The correct response is (a) alone, and Bisanz et al. argued that only subjects who selected this reponse would be responding on the basis of the analogical "rule" (the relation "+2").

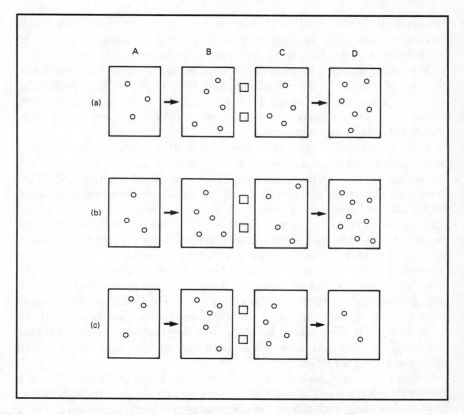

FIG. 4.3. The Dot Analogy Task (reproduced with permission from Bisanz et al., 1984).

Children aged 9, 11 and 13 years and college students took part in the study. Prior to receiving the dot analogies, the children were trained with eight geometric analogies. During this training, they were told about the relational similarity constraint. The experimenter explained that the problems were correct "... if the change from the first to second parts is the same as the change from the third to fourth parts" (p. 167). These instructions were intended to make the children realise that they needed to think about both magnitude *and* direction when solving the analogies.

Subsequent performance with the dot analogies showed that the ability to consider both magnitude and direction in combination (i.e. to extract the analogical "rule") improved with age. None of the 9-year-olds responded on the basis of the combined attributes, compared to 45% of the 11-year-olds, 57% of the 13-year-olds and 89% of the college students.

However, the children did not seem to respond on the basis of a single attribute when they made mistakes. Only 5% of the responses for the 9-year-olds and 6% for the 11-year-olds were based on the attributes of either magnitude or direction alone. Instead, 60% of the 9-year-olds said that all of the analogies were false, and 35% produced "unclassifiable" response strategies. It seems probable that the younger children were responding on the basis of quite different relations than those being measured by the experimenters.

In an effort to find out what these alternative relations were, Bisanz et al. conducted a second study in which they asked a subset of the 9-year-olds in the "all false" group to solve some more dot analogies. This time they asked the children to justify their responses to each problem. Some of the 11-year-olds who had shown evidence of the "all false" strategy were included as well. The "all false" responders turned out to be using relations that were quite unconnected with the attributes of magnitude and direction. Two strategies could be consistently identified. The most frequent was the *addition* strategy, in which the analogies were judged as correct if A+B = C+D (e.g. 4:3::6:1). Another popular strategy was the *match* strategy, in which the analogies were judged to be correct if one term matched another in quantity (e.g. if B = D, or if A = C). The match strategy was very robust, as the children persisted in using it even after training on the relations of both magnitude and direction.

Bisanz et al. suggested that the match strategy could be seen as a numerical version of the associative strategy used by younger children in verbal analogy tasks. Because the younger children persisted in using the addition and the match strategies, they concluded that they "failed to understand the conceptual constraints on analogy problems. ... Some subjects (especially 11-year-olds) recognised the need for arithmetic operations, and most recognised the need to match some quantity with another quantity, but apparently no one understood the requirement that a transformation (A–B) be matched with another transformation (C–D)" (pp. 173–174). So once again, we find experimenters reaching the conclusion that younger children do not understand the relational similarity constraint.

However, as is so frequently the case, it is impossible to distinguish between a failure to understand relational similarity and a failure to extract the appropriate relations in this experiment. Although most 9-year-olds can understand relations like "+2" without difficulty, their persistent use of the addition and the match strategies suggests that they did not realise that these relations were intended to be the basis of the analogies. In fact, they *were* trying to make the two halves of the analogies correspond, as both the addition and the match strategies were based on a comparison of the arithmetic attributes of the two halves of the problems. Unfortunately, as Bisanz et al. pointed out, the children were not equating the arithmetic transformations, and so they were solving the analogies incorrectly. Such errors, however, do not provide unambiguous evidence of a failure to understand the relational similarity constraint.

## Training Children to Use the Component Steps

Let us conclude our survey of the information-processing literature by considering some research that paints a more positive picture of young children's analogical abilities. Although most information-processing research has focused on older children, Alexander and her group have recently extended the componential approach to study analogical reasoning in preschoolers. They were interested in whether 3- and 4-year-olds could use the different components of analogical reasoning, and in particular whether it was possible to *teach* such young children to use these different components. Clearly, if very young children can learn to use the component steps, then they cannot be cognitively incapable of understanding the relational similarity constraint. Alexander and her colleagues have developed a training technique suitable for children as young as 3 years of age to study this question (e.g. Alexander et al., 1989).

Their training technique is based on the Geometric Analogies Test (the GAT), which was designed to provide a simple test of analogical reasoning (Alexander, Willson, White & Fuqua, 1987a). The test is based on plastic blocks that vary along three dimensions: *colour* (red, blue, yellow), *shape* (rectangle, square, circle, triangle) and *size* (large and small). These blocks can be used to create a variety of analogies that vary in the number of A:B transformations along the three dimensions. For example, the AB pair *large red circle:small red circle* varies only on the *size* dimension, whereas the AB pair *large red circle:small blue circle* varies on both the *colour* and the *size* dimensions. Each item on the GAT also has three distractors (i.e. A:B::C: D1, D2, D3, $D_{true}$).

In a typical training study, the GAT is first used as a basis for selecting children for componential training. For example, in Alexander et al. (1989), 60 children aged 4–5 years were given the GAT, and 50 of them were classified as non-analogical reasoners (these children all scored at chance or less on the test). Of these 50 non-analogical reasoners, 20 were then trained to use the components of analogical reasoning. The remaining 30 children formed an untrained control group.

Training began with the experimenters articulating the processes of *encoding, inferring, mapping* and *application* through the construction of concrete analogies based on toy cars or toy farm animals. A typical concrete analogy would be *red sports car:red hot rod::blue sports car:blue hot rod*, as depicted in Fig. 4.4. To train *encoding*, the experimenter gave a detailed description of the A and the B terms in the analogy (she explained that they were both red convertible cars). To train *inferring*, the experimenter described how the A and the B terms were both similar and different (e.g. she explained that both were red convertible cars, but that one was a sports car and one was a "hot rod"). Encoding of the C term followed (the blue sports car), and training in *mapping* then took place, with the experimenter explaining that the child should think about how the A and the C terms went together (both were sports cars, but one was blue and one was red, so their colours differed). Finally, to train *application*, the experimenter explained that to play the game the child had to find a toy car that went with the C term in the same way as the A and the B terms went together (the relational similarity constraint). In this example, the child had to select a blue "hot rod". The children were then given experience of solving some concrete analogies, helped by corrective feedback from the experimenter.

Following training with these concrete analogies, a second session of training was given using more abstract analogy items such as tree shapes (see Fig. 4.5). A third training session used the plastic attribute blocks from the GAT, although different problems from those used in the pre-test were given. Finally, the standard form of the GAT was administered to both the trained and the untrained groups on five further test sessions, each of these being given a month apart.

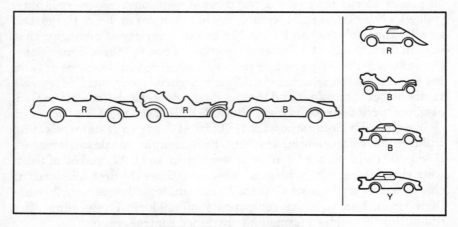

FIG. 4.4. A concrete analogy (reproduced with permission from Alexander et al., 1989).

FIG. 4.5. An abstract analogy (reproduced with permission from Alexander et al., 1989).

If 4- and 5-year-old children can learn to use the different components of analogical reasoning, then we would expect a difference in the performance of the trained and the untrained groups in the five post-tests with the GAT. Analysis of this post-test performance showed that the trained group were significantly better than their controls at solving geometric analogies from the second test session onwards, even though the two groups had not differed in their initial analogical ability (all were non-analogical reasoners). So training in the use of the different components had an immediate and sustained effect on analogical performance. By the fifth testing session, the trained group were performing as well as the children who were originally classified as analogical reasoners. Similar improvement following training has also been demonstrated with even younger children (e.g. Alexander et al., 1987b, in a study with gifted 3-year-olds).

These are impressive results. Alexander and her group have demonstrated that even 3- and 4-year-old children can use the different component processes of analogical reasoning if they are taught how to do so, and that such training has a beneficial effect on their ability to reason by analogy in the GAT. However, these studies do not enable us to decide *which* components of analogical reasoning have the greatest impact on performance. It is possible that training with only one or two of the components (such as inference and application) could cause equivalent improvements in analogical reasoning. Alexander et al.'s technique could easily be adjusted to make such comparisons between the different components.

### Training Inference and Application

The question of whether the inference and the application components are responsible for most of the training effects is theoretically very important given the correspondence between these components and our factors of relational knowledge and knowledge of the relational similarity constraint. In fact, the results of a training study with slightly older children (5-, 6- and 7-year-olds) supports the idea that training on the inference and the application components is sufficient to benefit analogy performance (Nippold & Sullivan, 1987).

Nippold and Sullivan's study used a picture version of the A:B::C:D task. The first step was to train the children on the inference and the application components with four practice items. A typical item would be *rabbit:carrot::boy: sandwich*, *girl*, *bicycle*, as shown in Fig. 4.6. Training consisted of a verbal explanation of each component. The experimenter explained:

> These two pictures go together, rabbit and carrot. Do you know why they go together? ... It's because the rabbit *eats* the carrot (*inference*). Now something goes with the boy. See if you can find it down here ... it's the sandwich, because the boy *eats* the sandwich (*application*). You see? ... The rabbit eats the carrot and the boy eats the sandwich ... so rabbit goes with carrot and boy goes with sandwich (p. 370).

In the test phase of the study, the experimenter presented new items for the children to solve unaided, again naming the pictures in each analogy for the children. For example, the experimenter would say "*Comb* goes with *hair*, and *rake* goes with ... is it *shovel, lawnmower* or *grass*?" while pointing to the pictures, which were arranged in a 2 x 2 matrix with an empty cell. The possible solution pictures were placed in a row beneath the matrix, and the two distractors were both associates of the C term. So in the test phase, the children had to come up with the appropriate relation to solve the analogy, and they also had to apply the relational similarity constraint.

Following the relatively short training period (four items), Nippold and Sullivan found that even the 5-year-olds performed well with the new picture analogies, solving 50% of them correctly. The 6- and 7-year-olds solved 62% and 67% of the new analogies, respectively. So

FIG. 4.6. A picture analogy (Nippold & Sullivan, 1987. Reprinted with permission of the American Speech-Language-Hearing Association.).

training on inference and application does seem to promote successful analogical reasoning. Although this experiment did not include a comparison with an untrained control group, these performance levels are impressive given the previous literature.

### "Near" vs "Far" Training Effects

The final question that needs to be asked about training concerns its generalisability. If training children to use the component steps of analogical reasoning can improve their analogical skills, then componential training should generalise to all kinds of analogies. In the studies described so far, however, both training and testing have been based on the same stimuli (either the attribute blocks in the GAT, or the picture analogies). The worry is thus that the effects of training might be highly specific. The children may simply be learning how to succeed on the GAT, or with the picture analogies.

To see whether training also leads to more general learning about analogy, we need a study in which completely different kinds of analogies are used in the training and testing phases. In fact, Alexander herself has designed a study that partially meets these criteria. She has trained children with three different kinds of analogies—pictorial analogies, verbal analogies (such as *airplane:bird::submarine:?*) and textual analogies—in which children read passages of text and then have to make analogical comparisons (e.g. *Why are astronauts like the pioneers of the Old West?*).

In one such study with 9-year-old children (Alexander, White, Haensly & Crimmins-Jeanes, 1987c), training began with the pictorial analogies (e.g. *horse:foal::cow:?*), and then progressed to the verbal and textual analogies. The training method was similar to that used with younger children. *Encoding* was trained by showing the children each term in the analogy separately, and asking them to explain their understanding of each one. *Inferring* was trained by asking the children to generate possible relations between the A and the B terms (prior to seeing the C term), and *mapping* was trained by asking the children to generate relations between the A and the C terms. *Application* was trained by asking the children to generate possible responses (D terms) to the analogy, and also to provide a rationale for them. Verbal and textual analogies were used to practise the different components. Finally, the children took part in a review and discussion session about analogies and the component processes.

To assess the effects of the training, all of the children were pre-tested with 30 verbal analogies of the form A:B::C:? before training, and were post-tested with 30 different verbal analogies immediately afterwards. This post-test was repeated 6 weeks later. A control group that had received no training was also given these pre-tests and post-tests. Alexander et al. found that the children who had been trained on the components of analogical reasoning solved significantly more analogies compared to this control group at both the immediate and the delayed post-tests, even though the two groups had shown the same analogical ability at pre-test. In a second study with older children (13- and 15-year-olds), two different post-tests were used, the verbal analogy items from Study 1 and a measure in which only the first two terms of the stem were provided (e.g. A:B:: ?:?). Similar training effects were found.

These studies of transfer go some way towards reassuring us that training in the component processes generalises to different kinds of analogies. The children showed analogical transfer from the pictorial to the verbal analogies, and also to verbal analogies presented in a different format. Alexander et al. describe the verbal analogy tests as "near" tests of transfer, as similar verbal analogies were used in the training sessions. They also designed what they describe as a "far" test of transfer. This was a test of "inferential ability", in which the children were required to comprehend graduated passages of text by making inferences that enabled them to answer a series of questions about the passages. The "far" transfer measure was intended to provide a better test of the generalisability of training. However, Alexander et al. found that in this test, the training group did not out-perform their controls.

Does this mean that training on the component processes does not generalise? This is certainly one interpretation of Alexander et al.'s result. However, making inferences about text passages may not be a very good test of analogical transfer. It seems to involve rather different processes from the classical analogy task. Perhaps a better test of transfer would be to give the children reasoning problems to solve by analogy, problems which could also be presented in passages of text if necessary. We will look at this measure of analogical reasoning in the next chapter. In the meantime, it can be concluded that componential training may be rather specific in its effects on analogical reasoning.

## Summary

Information-processing analyses of children's analogical reasoning have in general provided converging evidence for the importance of relational knowledge in successful analogising. They have also confirmed that even very young children can use the relational similarity constraint if they understand the relations on which an analogy is based. Studies such as those by Nippold and Sullivan (1987) and by Alexander and her colleagues have supported the idea that even very young children can reason by analogy, and have shown that even 3- and 4-year-olds can be trained to use the components of analogical reasoning proposed by Sternberg's model. So research within the information-processing approach supports the cognitive–developmental research covered in earlier chapters in providing us with positive evidence for early analogical competence.

CHAPTER FIVE

# Problem Analogies and Analogical Development

Research using the problem analogy paradigm provides a refreshing change from the deficit notions of analogical development found in the traditional classical/information-processing analogy literature. Researchers who use problem analogies are aware that the absence of the relevant relational knowledge will prevent successful analogical reasoning. Their interest has focused instead on *when* children will use the relational similarity constraint, and on *how* this interacts with the extraction of relations. So instead of worrying about competence, researchers studying problem analogies have sought to discover the *performance* factors governing children's use of analogy.

In problem analogy experiments, children are required to solve new problems (called "target" problems) by analogy to model problems (called "base" problems). They usually learn about the base by listening to a story about a protagonist with a problem (the story-mapping task). The important question is whether they will recognise the relational correspondence between the base and the target, and use an analogy based on the protagonist's solution to solve the target problem. It is important to notice that whereas in classical analogies the need to reason by analogy is made explicit in the paradigm, in problem analogies this is not the case. The child has to notice that an analogy is appropriate as well as to extract the relations relevant to the analogy.

Researchers quickly discovered that although even very young children could apply analogies to solve problems, they were not very good at recognising when an analogy was useful. They also had difficulty in disembedding the analogical relations from the base problem, a difficulty that frequently prevented them from noticing the analogy in the first place. Research thus concentrated on discovering which factors helped children to use analogies. A variety of different factors turned out to influence children's performance when the problem domain was familiar, and these factors all seemed to operate in one of two ways. They either helped the children to realise that an analogy was appropriate, or they helped the children to extract the relations on which the analogy was based. These outcomes are of course not independent. Sometimes a hint that an analogy is appropriate will lead a child to focus on relational structure, and sometimes instructions designed to disembed relational structure will help the child to use an analogy.

In this chapter, I will consider different performance factors in the approximate order of the degree of facilitation that they provide in children's analogical reasoning. This approximate "facilitation gradient" is complicated by the fact that some studies have used a combination of performance factors, and that most factors do not operate independently of each other. Although the discussion will only consider research with children, it is important to realise that exactly the same factors seem to facilitate analogical reasoning in adults (see, for example, Gick & Holyoak, 1980, 1983; Holyoak & Koh, 1987). Since the same factors can be shown to affect the performance of both children and adults in the same ways, it is unlikely that analogical *competence* is being altered in these studies.

## PERFORMANCE FACTORS IN ANALOGICAL PROBLEM-SOLVING

### 1. Providing Hints to Use Analogy

One way to affect analogical performance is to hint to the children that an analogy can help them to solve their problem. The effect of hints on analogical performance was first investigated in a landmark study of problem analogies carried out by Holyoak et al. (1984). Holyoak and his colleagues pioneered the use of the story-mapping paradigm with children, and the stories that they designed have been used in much subsequent research.

In Holyoak et al.'s study, the target problem was to transfer some small rubber balls from one bowl on a table (placed within reach) to another bowl farther away (and out of reach). Various tools were available to help the children to solve this problem, including scissors, string, a large sheet of heavy paper, an aluminium cane and a cardboard tube. The children, who were aged 4–6 and 11–12 years, were required to devise as many ways as possible of moving the rubber balls without leaving their seats.

Before receiving this target problem, some of the children were told a story about a genie who had to solve a similar problem involving the transfer of some precious jewels from one bottle to another. There were two story analogues—the "Magic Carpet" analogy and the "Magic Staff" analogy—and both stories were accompanied by pictures. In the former, the genie solved his problem by commanding his magic carpet to roll itself into a tube. He then rolled his jewels through this tube into the second bottle. In the latter, the genie solved the transportation problem by using his magic staff to pull the new bottle over to the side of the old bottle, bringing it near enough to transfer the jewels. The analogous solutions for the children were meant to be to roll the sheet of paper into a tube and then to roll the balls through it, or to use the aluminium cane to bring the far bowl towards the near bowl so that they could transfer the balls. The intended analogical correspondences between the base stories and the target are shown in Table 5.1.

The children's ability to think of the analogous solutions was measured both prior to and after receiving a hint that the genie's story could help them, and the solutions that they generated were compared to those of a control group who did not hear the genie stories before

TABLE 5.1

The Analogous Correspondences in the Problems used by Holyoak et al. (1984)[a]

|  | Story Analogues | Ball Problem |
|---|---|---|
| **Initial state:** | | |
| Goal ............. | Genie wishes to transfer jewels from one bottle to another. | Child wishes to transfer balls from one bowl to another. |
| Resources .... | Magic staff/magic carpet. | Walking cane/sheet of paper. |
| Constraint ..... | Must not drop or lose jewels. | Must not drop or lose any balls. |
| Solution plan 1 | Genie *(a)* uses magic staff to pull goal bottle closer to initial bottle; *(b)* drops jewels into goal bottle. | Child *(a)* uses cane to pull goal bowl closer to initial bowl; (b) drops balls into goal bowl. |
| Solution plan 2 | Genie *(a)* rolls magic carpet to form a long hollow tube; (b) places tube so it extends from initial bottle to goal bottle; (c) rolls jewels through tube to goal bottle | Child *(a)* rolls sheet of paper to form long hollow tube; *(b)* places tube so it extends from initial bowl to goal bowl; *(c)* rolls balls through tube to goal bottle. |
| Outcome .......... | Jewels are transferred safely. | Balls are transferred safely. |

[a] Reproduced with permission.

receiving the target problem. Holyoak et al. found that some of the younger children could use both analogies spontaneously. Fifty percent of them used the cane solution in the Magic Staff problem before receiving the hint compared to only one child in the control group (10%), and in the Magic Carpet analogy 30% of them rolled up the paper (compared again to 10% of the controls). The effect of the hint differed dramatically in the two analogies, however. In the Magic Staff problem, all of the children used the analogy following the hint, whereas in the Magic Carpet problem the hint had no effect on performance at all. In contrast, the older children *did* benefit from the hint in the Magic Carpet analogy: All of them used the analogy after receiving a hint, whereas only 30% had made an analogy spontaneously. None of the older control subjects thought of the rolling solution.

The finding that the younger children failed to benefit from the hint in the Magic Carpet analogy is surprising. Holyoak et al.'s explanation of this unexpected result was that the magic carpet and the sheet of paper were perceptually and functionally less similar than the magic staff and the aluminium cane. This lack of perceptual similarity between the carpet and the sheet of paper made it difficult to use the hint and transfer the "rolling" solution in the Magic Carpet analogy, whereas the high perceptual similarity between the cane and the magic staff made it easy for the younger children to use the hint and transfer the "pulling" solution in the Magic Staff analogy. We will return to the role of perceptual similarity in analogical performance later in this chapter. For now, we will simply conclude that hints to use analogy do not always help children to notice relational correspondences.

## 2. The Presentation of More than One Analogy

Another way to make children realise that analogies are appropriate to their overall goal of problem solving is to give them more than one example of an analogous solution. The provision of multiple analogies may help them to notice that an analogy is relevant to their task. As with hints, providing more than one analogy does not explicitly help the children to extract the relational structure of the base problem, but it may help them to notice the analogy in the first place. This may in turn affect the extraction of relational similarity.

Evidence that two analogies *are* better than one for promoting transfer has come from a number of studies. For example, Gholson, Eymard, Morgan and Kamhi (1987) gave 9- and 12-year-old children an analogue of the "Farmer's Dilemma" problem to solve. In the Farmer's Dilemma, a farmer has to transport a fox, a goose and some corn across a river using a boat that will hold only two passengers. If the goose and the corn share the boat, the goose will eat the corn, whereas if the goose and the fox share the boat, the fox will eat the goose. The problem is to get all the animals and the corn safely across the river, and the most efficient solution takes seven moves.

The target problem for the children was to get a lion, a pony and some oats across a canyon without the lion eating the pony or the pony eating the oats. The children either tried to solve this target problem after learning the solution to the Farmer's Dilemma, or after learning about *both* the Farmer's Dilemma and an analogous problem concerning a wolf, a rabbit, some carrots and a mountain. The children who had learned two analogies solved the target problem in significantly fewer moves than those who had learned only one analogy. So receiving two analogies clearly benefited transfer. However, this could either have been due to the increased salience of the analogy, or to extra practice with the solution. A control condition in which some children received the *same* analogy twice would help us to decide whether the extra improvement found with two analogies was simply a function of practice.

One reason that an analogy may become more salient following a greater variety of examples is that children who are given more analogies may extract a more generalised solution schema for solving a problem than those who only learn about one analogy. Comparing and contrasting analogies may help in disembedding relational structure. To compare whether such generalised solution schemas led to better analogical transfer than more specific representations of solution principles, Chen and Daehler (1989) designed a study to measure the effect of the subjects' representational level of the solution principle on their analogical performance. They expected that children who were able to extract more "abstract" representations of solution principles would make more analogies. Children who remembered the specific information in the analogies (e.g. about foxes and geese, or about wolves and rabbits) might not show transfer, even if they had learned multiple analogies.

In their experiment, Chen and Daehler gave two groups of children a target problem in which they had to extract a bead from a narrow glass cylinder. The cylinder was 12" deep but only 2" wide, and the bead was floating in a small amount of water at the bottom. The dimensions of the cylinder, which the children were not allowed to invert, prevented them from simply reaching in and extracting the bead. Instead, they were encouraged to use various tools to reach the bead, including scissors, a hammer, two sticks, a short spoon and a cup of extra water.

Two extraction solutions were actually possible. One solution involved adding more water to the cylinder until the bead floated to the top, and the other required the children to combine one of the sticks with the spoon to make a tool to scoop out the bead. However, for one group of children the amount of water in the cup was actually insufficient to bring the ball high enough up the cylinder for it to be successfully extracted, while for the other group the spoon lacked a connector that enabled it to be attached to the stick. This meant that the former group could only solve the target problem by using the spoon (the *combining* solution), while the latter group had to add water to the cylinder (the *adding* solution).

The children, who were 6-year-olds, were told two stories prior to receiving the target problem. These stories either provided analogies for the adding solution or for the combining solution. For example, in one adding story, a ping-pong ball had fallen into a hole, and was retrieved by pouring some water into the hole. In one combining story, a monkey had to reach some food placed outside his cage, and joined two sticks together to do so. Chen and Daehler's idea was that after receiving two adding or combining analogies, the children would form an abstract solution schema that they could use to solve their problem with the bead.

If the representational level of the solution principle governs success in extracting the bead, then children who have extracted an abstract schema from the two stories should be significantly more likely to solve the target problem than those who have not. To measure this representational level, Chen and Daehler questioned each child about how the two base stories were similar. The children's responses were then scored for whether they had extracted "abstract" schemas or not. For example, a child who had recalled the goal structure of each story in terms of story-specific features would receive a lower score than a child who had generated a schema integrating the key elements and the solution principle for both stories. Chen and Daehler found a significant connection between this measure of abstractness and the successful solution of the target problem. All of the children who had extracted abstract solution schemas showed analogical transfer, compared to only 38% of those who had not. So receiving more than one analogy did seem to help some children to extract a generalised solution schema.

## 3. Positive *vs* Negative Analogies

Another interesting aspect of multiple analogies is that they have the potential to be misleading. If children draw the *wrong* analogy from prior examples, then this should actively prevent them from thinking of an appropriate solution to the target problem. So while abstract solution schemas can clearly benefit problem solving, it is also possible that they could impede it. To test this possibility, Chen and Daehler went on to vary the valency of the analogies in the experiment discussed above. Some of the children in their study were given *positive* analogies to the target problem, and others were given *negative* analogies. For example, a positive analogy might be hearing the adding stories in the situation where the cup had sufficient water to enable an analogous solution, whereas a negative analogy might be hearing the adding stories in the situation where it did not. Children who heard the adding stories but could only use the combining solution were expected to be hampered in their ability to solve the target problem, and vice versa.

As they had predicted, Chen and Daehler found that the children who had heard positive story analogies performed significantly better on the target problems than the children in a control group who had heard neutral base stories. Sixty percent of the positive analogy children solved the target problem, compared to 29% of this control group. The children who had heard negative story analogies performed more poorly on the target problem than the children in the control group, with only 8% solving the bead problem. So the negative analogies impeded the children's ability to generate the correct solution to the target problem. Being taught misleading analogies can make problem solving more difficult.

The demonstration that analogy can have negative as well as positive effects on reasoning is a particularly important one. In many situations of everyday reasoning, people will possess knowledge that actually *prevents* them from solving problems. One context in which these negative analogies can be very problematic is in the classroom (see also Chapter 7). Such worries are quite realistic, as was recently demonstrated by Lamsfuss and Wilkening (1991) in a study of children's reasoning about physical forces.

To examine young children's understanding of "intuitive physics", Lamsfuss and Wilkening had asked them to solve a problem that involved getting a "king" into his "royal bed". The king (a solid object) was in the centre of a table, and had two forces attached to him, both consisting of weighted strings. The children had to position the royal bed so that the king would be propelled into it when the forces were released. The experimental apparatus is depicted in Fig. 5.1.

Most of the younger children (7- to 10-year-olds) put the royal bed into the wrong position. They mistakenly assumed that only the stronger force (the heavier weight) had to be considered in working out the eventual resting place of the king. This misconception apparently arose from a "self-initiated" analogy to a balance scale, which many of the children spontaneously mentioned while they were reasoning about the king. In a balance scale, only the heavier weight goes down, and so only one weight has to be considered, whereas in the force situation both

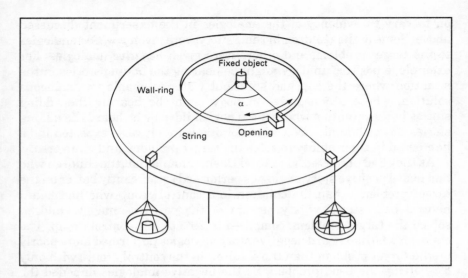

FIG. 5.1. The apparatus designed by Lamsfuss and Wilkening (1991). Reproduced with permission.

weights go down, and so they must both be taken into account. The false analogy with the balance scale apparently led the children to use erroneous "one-force-only" strategies in positioning the royal bed.

In contrast, the older children tended to use the correct "two-forces-considered" strategy in their reasoning. Lamsfuss and Wilkening wondered whether learning about the misleading balance scale analogy could lead the older children away from this correct strategy and towards the erroneous "one-force-only" strategy. To examine this question, they decided to teach a new group of older children about the balance scale. Some of them learned a traditional balance scale task, in which only the heavier weight needed to be considered (a negative analogy), whereas others learned a modified balance scale task, in which both weights had to be considered (a positive analogy). The former group were expected to be poorer at solving the problem with the king.

Lamsfuss and Wilkening found that the children who had received the negative analogy were more likely subsequently to use erroneous "one-force-only" strategies in positioning the royal bed compared to a control group, whereas those who had received the positive analogy were more likely to use a correct "two-forces-considered" strategy. In the former case, 87% of the children trained with the negative analogy used a "one-force-only" strategy, compared to 45% of the control group, whereas in the latter case 31% of the children trained with the positive analogy used a "one-force-only" strategy. So even children who were capable of reasoning appropriately could be influenced by false analogies. It is clearly important to find out more about self-initiated analogies, as they may interfere with many types of learning.

## 4. Explicit Prompts to Extract Relational Structure

So far we have considered performance factors that affect the likelihood that children will realise that analogies might be useful in solving problems. Hints to use analogy, or the provision of a number of positive (or negative) analogies, can alert children to the presence of a particular analogy (perhaps to the detriment of their problem-solving performance), but hints or multiple analogies will only affect *noticing* the analogy. To *use* the analogy, the children must extract the relational similarities between the base and the target problems, and this is something that many children seem to find difficult. So there are two hurdles in analogical problem solving. The first is noticing the relevant analogy, and the second is applying it.

The factors that affect application are those that help children to disembed the relational structure of a problem from its context. If the children have not represented the relations relevant to the analogy conceptually, then they are unlikely to apply it to solve new problems. This disembedding of relations may require more specific help from the experimenter than the provision of hints or multiple analogies. Research conducted by Brown and her colleagues has tried to determine how such disembedding is best achieved, and they have found that a variety of different methods can be successful (e.g. Brown & Kane, 1988; Brown, Kane & Echols, 1986; Brown, Kane & Long, 1989). They have also shown that once the children have managed to disembed the appropriate relational structure from the base problem, then noticing the analogy seldom presents any difficulty.

### The Provision of Instructions

One way to help children to disembed relational structure is to tell them to use an analogy. In some studies that extended Holyoak et al.'s "Magic Carpet" paradigm, Brown et al. (1989) examined the effect of explicit instructions on analogical transfer. Their experimental technique was based on story-mapping. Brown et al. were interested in children's ability to transfer the "rolling" solution from an analogous base problem *to* the Genie Problem.

In their study, the children (7-year-olds) were first given the Genie Problem (the target) to try to solve without any help from the experimenter. The problem was presented via a toy scenario and toy props. If they were unsuccessful, as they usually were, the Genie Problem was put to one side, and the children were told that they would work on an easier problem (the base) that would help them to solve the Genie's Problem. They were told "Let's just tell the genie that we won't forget, that we'll be back later after we have learned how to help him". The easier problem was either about an Easter bunny or a farmer. The Easter bunny had to move some eggs across a river, and the farmer had to move some cherries across a fallen tree. Toy scenarios were again provided. The different stories used by Brown et al. are shown in Table 5.2.

When the children also failed to solve this second problem, the experimenter showed them an illustrated book of the story that demonstrated the solution. She showed the children that the Easter bunny solved his problem by rolling his blanket into a tube and then

TABLE 5.2
The Analogous Problems used by Brown et al. (1986)[a]

**Problem 1. The Genie**
A magic genie lived for many years in a field behind a wall. His home was a very pretty bottle where he lived happily and collected a fine set of jewels. But one day an envious witch put a spell on the genie. He was stuck to the spot, he couldn't move his feet, all his magic powers were gone. If he could move his home to the other side of the wall, he would be out of reach of the spell and his magic would come back. He had found an even prettier larger bottle on the other side, but he has a problem. How can he get his jewels across the high wall into the new bottle without breaking them and without moving his feet? The genie has all these treasures to help him (glue, string, tape, etc.). Can you think of any way the genie can get his jewels into the new bottles?

**Problem 2. The Rabbit**
Here is the Easter bunny's problem. The Easter bunny has to deliver all these Easter eggs to all the little children before Easter (tomorrow), but he has been working so hard all week, painting the eggs and hiding them for Easter egg hunts. He would really like to rest and to stay here with his friends and have a picnic. If he stays, he won't have time to finish delivering the eggs. The Easter bunny has finished delivering all the eggs on this side of the river (points to picnic side), but he hasn't started on the other side. The Easter bunny has a rabbit friend on the other side of the river who has offered to help him (points to second rabbit waiting with an empty basket on the other side of the river), but how can the Easter bunny get the eggs across the river into his friend's basket? The river is big, there are no bridges or boats, and rabbits can't swim and don't like to get wet. What can he do? Can you think of anything he could use to get the eggs to the helpful bunny?

**Problem 3. The Farmer**
Farmer Jones is very happy. He has picked a whole bunch of cherries and is taking them to market. When he sells them, he will have enough money to go on vacation with his family. They will go to the seaside. He wants to deliver the load of cherries to the market. That morning there is a great storm, with rain, thunder and lightning. But he cannot wait to take the cherries to market because the cherries are just ripe now and will go bad. On his way to market, he finds the road blocked by a very big fallen tree knocked over in the storm. What can he do? He must get his cherries to market quickly, otherwise they will go bad. A friend has driven his tractor up to the other side of the tree and will lend it to Farmer Jones, but how will he get the cherries across the big, big tree? He can't reach over, and he mustn't damage the cherries.

[a] Reproduced with permission.

rolling his eggs through it, or that the farmer solved his problem by rolling his rug into a tube and then rolling his cherries through it. The children were told that now they could help the genie, as the two problems were just the same, and were given a second try at solving the genie's problem. Various tools were provided to help the children to solve this target problem, including a sheet of paper, glue, string, etc., as in the Holyoak et al. study. A control group of children received the same sequence of problems, but without any of the explicit instructions to use analogy.

Brown et al. found that 46% of the *instructional analogy* group transferred the "rolling" solution to the target problem, compared to only 20% of the control group. This shows that the children were more likely to disembed the relational structure of the base problem when they had been told that it was relevant to do so. However, despite these instructions, the resulting transfer levels were fairly modest. The majority of the children in the experimental group (54%) did not extract the appropriate relations from the base problem, despite the explicit instructions that they had received from the experimenter.

*Highlighting the Goal Structure of the Story*
Another way to make children focus on the underlying relations in a story analogy is to purposely question them about the story's structure. Brown et al. (1986) used this technique in another series of studies based on Holyoak et al.'s "Magic Carpet" paradigm. This time they measured transfer *from* the Genie Problem to analogous problems.

In this set of experiments, younger children (4- and 5-year-olds) were told the standard genie story (the base) with the help of toy props, so that they could enact the "rolling" solution with the experimenter. As before, a large sheet of paper represented the carpet. The children were then questioned about the goal structure of the story. They were asked questions such as "Who has a problem?", "What did the genie need to do?", "What is stopping him?" and "How does he solve his problem?" These questions were designed to encourage the children to extract the genie's solution of "rolling" from the specific details of the story.

The children were then told another story about someone else with a problem, again via the use of toy scenarios and props, and were asked to solve this new (target) problem. The target problem was always about the Easter bunny, who had to move some eggs across a river. The sheet of paper was left out for the children to use in solving this new problem, and other tools (glue, string, etc.) were again provided. The ability of the children to solve the transfer problem was compared to that of a control group of children who had also heard the genie story, but who were not questioned about it.

Brown et al. found that performance was much better in the questioning condition (*explicit goal structure*), in which about 70% of the children solved the target problem by rolling up the sheet of paper, than in the control condition, where only 20% of the children spontaneously made the analogy with the rolling solution. This pattern of results was replicated in two further studies. So helping children to extract the goal structure of a story has a greater effect on their ability to apply analogies than simply instructing them about problem similarity (70% transfer *vs* 46% transfer). Once they have been helped to represent the relational structure of the base problem via questioning, then most children will notice its relational similarity to the target problem by themselves.

*"Learning-to-learn" Effects*
Is it possible to help children to represent relational structure in the story-mapping paradigm without explicitly questioning them about the goal structure of the stories? We know from Chen and Daehler's work that it is easier to represent relational structure if more than one analogy is provided. In their study, positive transfer with two analogies was at around 60%, which is almost as high as the transfer levels that resulted from Brown et al.'s explicit questioning technique. So children who receive a number of similar problems to solve are more likely to disembed and represent relations by themselves than children who are simply told about problem similarity by the experimenter (46% transfer). Clearly, therefore, the effect of giving children more than one analogy in addition to instructing them about problem similarity becomes of interest. With the help of both of these factors, it is possible that every child would show transfer. Brown et al. (1989) explored the effects of combining these two factors in a study using the same Easter bunny and farmer stories.

Their method involved using a staggered presentation of the "rolling" problems, a technique which they referred to as the "A–B–A–C paradigm". We have already discussed the first stage in their experiment. The children (7-year-olds) were first given the Genie Problem (problem A) to try to solve on their own, and were then given an easier problem (problem B: either Easter Bunny or Farmer) that they solved with the help of the experimenter. They then received the Genie Problem a second time (problem A2) to solve on their own. During this procedure, they were frequently told that problem B would help them to help the genie, as the two problems were just the same. After receiving problem A2, they were shown an illustrated story about the Genie's Problem that demonstrated the rolled carpet solution. In the final stage of the study, the remaining problem (problem C: either Farmer or Easter Bunny) was presented for the children to solve, this time without any instructions about problem similarity.

The important comparison was between a control group, who simply received the problems in the A–B–A–C sequence without any commentary from the experimenter (the standard multiple analogy paradigm), and the instructional analogy group, who received the same problem sequence accompanied by the instructions outlined above. Transfer in the experimental group was expected to be greater than in this control group, as the former group had received more than one analogy as well as some instruction about problem similarity. This was exactly what Brown et al. found. Analogical transfer to the third (C) problem was greater for the children in the instructional analogy group, 98% of whom rolled up the paper, than for the children in the control group, 39% of whom rolled up the paper. So the provision of multiple analogies in combination with explicit instructions about problem similarity can lead to (almost) perfect analogical transfer.

Brown et al. argued that their results showed a "learning-to-learn" effect. They pointed out that the enhanced performance shown by the experimental group was not a simple matter of providing instructions to use analogy (after all, the children were never told *how* the problems were alike). The use of more than one analogy had a noticeable (and independent) effect on successful transfer. With only one prior analogue, transfer to problem B in the instructional analogy group was at 46%, whereas with two prior analogues the children doubled their success rate to 98%. A similar enhancement was found in the control group. With one prior analogue, transfer was at 20%, whereas with two prior analogues it doubled to 39%. So if instructions are combined with multiple analogies, then children will learn that the problem-solving goal is to apply an analogous solution, and this "meta-knowledge" ("learning-to-learn") will help them to extract the relevant relational structure from the base problem and apply the analogy.

### Formation of a "Learning Set"

An important point about the A–B–A–C manipulation, however, is that the solution to be transferred is always the same one. This makes it difficult to differentiate between the children's ability to learn to disembed relational structure and their ability to learn that analogy is relevant. One obvious question thus remains, which is whether the multiple analogy technique can be used to engineer both spontaneous noticing that analogy is required, and spontaneous disembedding of the relevant relations. For this we need a paradigm in which different analogous solutions must be transferred during learning. Brown and Kane (1988) came up with a new story-mapping technique based on pairs of stories to study this question.

This new paradigm, which they called the "A1–A2, B1–B2, C1–C2 paradigm", required the children to learn two different things: to look for and apply analogous solutions, and to extract the relevant relational mappings in each problem pair for themselves. As each pair of problems required a different analogy, the children could not simply repeat the *same* analogy at each step of the paradigm. A more abstract notion of problem-solving-by-analogy had to be transferred between the problem pairs, and this required the formation of a "learning set" to seek analogies.

To measure the formation of a learning set, Brown and Kane decided to devise some new problems. These were based on the relations of *stacking* (e.g. stacking hay bales or tyres to reach something high up), *swinging* (e.g. using a tree branch or a telephone wire to swing over a divide) and *pulling* (e.g. using a spade or a fishing rod to pull someone to safety). An individual child might have to make an analogy based on *stacking* for problem A2, an analogy based on *pulling* for problem B2 and an analogy based on *swinging* for problem C2. After solving each problem pair, the children were asked to say how the problems in the pair were alike. The story pairs that Brown and Kane used are shown in Table 5.3.

Brown and Kane were most interested in the children's performance on the second C problem (C2). They argued that if the children were picking up the abstract notion of problem-solving-by-analogy (forming a "learning set"), then this would become evident by the third problem pair. In fact, almost all of the children in the study formed a learning set. Problem C2 was solved by approximately 85% of the 3-year-olds, 95% of the 4-year-olds, and 100% of the 5-year-olds. A control group who received only the third problem pair (C1–C2) showed markedly poorer transfer (12%, 30% and 65% solving problem C2 at ages 3, 4 and 5 years respectively). So juxtaposing analogies in a way that promotes the formation of a learning set leads to excellent levels of transfer. Children can both disembed the appropriate relational structure to apply the analogy *and* notice that analogies are relevant, without explicit instruction about either noticing or application.

However, although this experiment did not involve explicit instruction about relational similarity, Brown and Kane did ask the children to explain how each pair of problems were alike, and this may also have helped to promote analogical transfer. A control condition was thus included in the experiment, in which explicit reflection on the similarity between the problem solutions was not required. Performance in this control condition showed that the transfer levels of the older children were relatively unaffected by the reflection manipulation. Transfer levels without reflection were 85% for the 4-year-olds and 100%

## TABLE 5.3
### The Story Pairs from the Learning Set Paradigm[a]

**Problem Set 1: Stacking**
A.  John (Jean), the garage mechanic, has a problem. He needs to take all of the tyres that have been delivered to his garage and put them up on a shelf. But the shelf is too high and he doesn't have a ladder, so he can't reach the shelf by himself. How can he solve his problem: *Solution:* Stack two tyres and stand on top of them.
B.  Bill (Brenda), the farmer, has a problem. He needs to put his bales of hay on top of his tractor so he can take them to the market. But Bill isn't tall enough to reach the top of the tractor by himself. How can he solve his problem? *Solution:* Stack two bales of hay and stand on top of them.

**Problem Set 2: Pulling**
A.  Mrs (Mr) Smith is a lady who grows flowers. One day she is working in her garden, removing weeds (with a hoe) when she hears a little boy crying. She looks up and sees that the little boy has fallen down a big hole at the bottom of her garden. She can't reach him because the ground around the hole will give way. How can Mrs Smith help? *Solution:* Mrs Smith sticks out her hoe, the boy grabs it, and he is pulled up.
B.  Linda (Steven), the girl guide, has a problem. She is fishing (with a pole) when suddenly she sees that a boat with a little girl in it has broken away from the dock and is floating downstream. She has to get the little girl and the boat back to shore. How can Linda solve her problem? *Solution:* Linda holds out her fishing pole and has the little girl grab it, and she pulls the boat to shore.

**Problem Set 3: Swinging**
A.  Carolyn (Carl), the nurse, has a problem. Earlier in the day when the water wasn't deep she walked across the stream to go visit a sick lady in the house on the other side. But while she was there, the weather got very bad, there was a big flood, and now the water is too deep and fast for her to walk, jump or swim across. She needs to get back to the other side before dark. How can she solve her problem? *Solution:* Grab onto a willow tree branch on the bank and swing across to the other side.
B.  Mr (Mrs) Brown, the telephone repairperson, has a problem. He is up on a roof to connect the telephone wires to the two telephone poles. He has all of his tools up there. Suddenly, he notices that the house is on fire. He needs to get to the roof on the other house to save himself. How can he solve his problem? *Solution:* Grab onto the telephone wires and swing across.

[a] Brown et al. (1989). Reprinted by permission of John Wiley & Sons Ltd.

for the 5-year-olds. These high levels of transfer were maintained in a second experiment in which the presentation of the stories was randomised (e.g. B1, A1, C1, A2, C2, B2). For the 3-year-olds, however, transfer levels without reflection were more modest. In this control condition, 40% of the 3-year-olds solved problem C2 correctly, compared to 85% in the reflection condition. So in the A1–A2, B1–B2, C1–C2 paradigm, 4- and 5-year-olds can abstract the relational similarities between analogous problems for themselves once they have picked up the abstract idea of problem-solving-by-analogy. Three-year-olds need the added support of being explicitly told to reflect on the similarity of the solutions used in each problem pair to show high levels of transfer.

## 5.  Superficial Similarities between Problems

A final factor that can affect analogical performance is the degree to which the objects in different problems share perceptual similarity. The possible role of this factor in analogical problem solving was raised earlier in our discussion of the original genie study by Holyoak et al. (1984). They had been surprised that a hint to use analogy had failed to benefit children's performance with the Magic Carpet analogy, and had noted that there was greater perceptual and functional similarity between the magic staff and the aluminium cane in their Magic Staff analogy than between the magic carpet and the sheet of paper in their Magic Carpet analogy. They proposed that this difference in superficial similarity could explain why the children only benefited from the hint in the Magic Staff analogy. If their idea is correct, then superficial similarities between problems should help children to notice analogies, and may help them to extract the appropriate relational similarities as well.

Superficial similarities could act as a support cue for relational reasoning in the following way. If the objects in the base and in the target problems are perceptually similar and also play similar roles in the problems, then matching similar objects will result in the alignment of similar relations, as relations are embedded in objects. So object similarity should help the children to sort out similarities in relational structure, and it may also help them to disembed the relational structure of a problem from its context. To test these possibilities, we need a study in which the same base problem can be used to solve target problems that vary in the degree of their perceptual similarity to the base.

The role of object similarity in children's analogical reasoning has long interested Gentner and her colleagues, and the experiment that comes closest to achieving this contrast was carried out by Gentner and Toupin (1986). They varied perceptual similarity in a story-mapping study that did not involve problem solving. In their study, they asked two groups of children aged 5–7 and 8–10 years to act out various stories with toy animal characters. The measure of analogy was to transfer the plot of each story from one set of animal characters to another *without* confusing its relational structure. For example, in the base story the hero might be a seal, his friend might be a penguin, and the villain might be a dog. In the transfer story, the hero might be a walrus, his friend might be a seagull, and the villain might be a cat. The child's job was to act out the story all over again, this time placing the walrus in the hero's role, the seagull in the friend's role, and the cat in the villain's role.

This mapping example is taken from the *high-similarity* condition in Gentner and Toupin's experiment, in which the animal characters in the different roles were chosen to be perceptually similar (i.e. hero:

seal/walrus; friend: penguin/seagull; villain: dog/cat). In a second *low-similarity* condition, the animals were chosen to be perceptually dissimilar (e.g. hero: seal/lion; friend: penguin/giraffe; villain: dog/camel), and in a third *cross-mapping* condition, the animals were perceptually similar but their roles in the story differed (e.g. hero in story 1: seal; friend in story 2: walrus). These different conditions are shown in Fig. 5.2. If superficial similarity cues help children to use relational structure, then the cross-mapping condition should be the most difficult for them, as here perceptual similarity conflicts with the required relational mappings.

Gentner and Toupin found that the children in both age groups showed a strong effect of perceptual similarity. They were better at mapping the stories in the high-similarity condition, with animals that were perceptually similar, than in the low-similarity condition, with animals that were perceptually dissimilar. The proportion of correct mappings in the former condition was around 90% for both age groups, whereas in the latter condition it was around 65% for the younger children and 85% for the older children. Both groups also performed most poorly in the cross-mapping condition, where perceptual similarity and relational similarity were in conflict. When perceptually-similar animals changed roles, the proportion of correct transfer was approximately 57% (young group) and 75% (older group) respectively. Gentner and Toupin concluded that "transparency"—the degree of perceptual similarity between the base and the target—influenced relational mappings between the stories for all of the children.

Does this imply that transparency will also affect problem-solving-by-analogy, with children finding it easier to use analogy when the objects in the analogical problems are perceptually similar? It seems likely that this would be the case, as such an effect has been demonstrated with adults (Holyoak & Koh, 1987). So far, however, there is only negative evidence that similar effects would occur with children. Ratterman, Gentner & Deloache (1987, in prep.) have shown that when perceptual similarity *conflicts* with relational similarity, then younger children's performance in problem-solving tasks will suffer.

Ratterman et al. demonstrated this effect in a search task based on the relation of relative size. In their task, the child and the experimenter each had a set of three objects, which were ordered by increasing size. The child's task was to find a sticker hidden under one of the objects in his or her array after having watched a sticker being hidden under an object in the experimenter's array. The rule was that the child's sticker would always be found under the object of the same *relative* size as that selected by the experimenter. For example, the experimenter might have an array of identical flower pots of sizes 1, 2 and 3, and the child

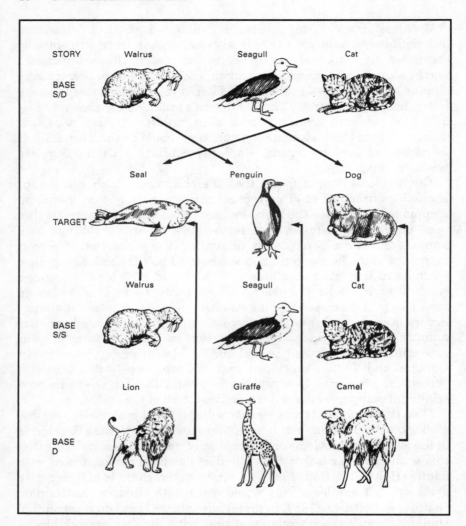

FIG. 5.2. The three story-mapping conditions used by Gentner and Toupin (1986). S/D, cross-mapping; S/S, high similarity; D, low similarity. Reproduced with permission.

might have an array of flower pots of sizes 2, 3 and 4. If the experimenter hid a sticker under pot 2 (middle size) in her array, then the child had to search under pot 3 (middle size) in his or her array in order to find the sticker (see Fig. 5.3).

To draw attention to the relational basis of the task, the children (3-year-olds) were first taught to apply the relational labels "Daddy", "Mommy" and "Baby" to toy animals that varied in size. They were then

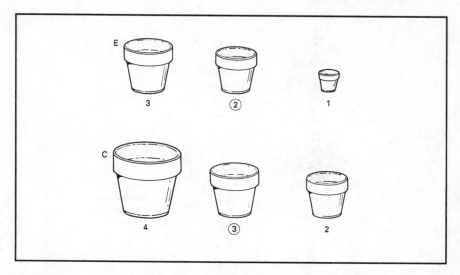

FIG. 5.3. The stimuli in the sparse condition (Ratterman et al., 1987). Reproduced with permission.

given the search task with the experimental stimuli. In the search task, they were asked questions such as "If I put my sticker under my Mommy, your sticker is under your Mommy. Look, my sticker is under my Mommy. Where do you think your sticker is?" These instructions were intended to make the relational size rule explicit.

To manipulate perceptual similarity, Ratterman et al. contrasted performance with the flower pots (dubbed the *sparse* condition) with performance with distinctive objects (the perceptually *rich* condition). In the rich condition, the different-sized objects were a large plastic flower (4), a medium toy house (3), a small coffee mug (2) and a very small toy car (1). Again, if the experimenter chose object 2 from her array of 2, 3 and 4 (i.e. the house), the child was meant to choose object 3 (the mug) from his or her array of 1, 2 and 3, as both were the middle-sized objects in the arrays. In the rich condition, the conflict between a wrong choice based on perceptual similarity (i.e. the other house—and large object) and the correct choice based on relational similarity (the middle-sized object—the mug) was much stronger than in the sparse condition. The stimuli for the rich condition are shown in Fig 5.4.

Ratterman et al. were interested in whether this conflict between perceptual similarity and relational similarity would impede the children's ability to reason about relative size. This turned out to be the case. Relational responding was significantly better in the sparse condition (81% relational responses), where the conflict with perceptual

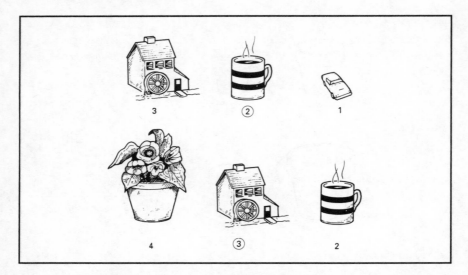

FIG. 5.4. The stimuli in the rich condition (Ratterman et al., 1987). Reproduced with permission.

similarity was weaker, than in the rich condition (50% relational responses), where the conflict between relational and object similarity was more marked. So when perceptual similarity conflicted with relational similarity, the children found it more difficult to respond on a relational basis.

How would they have fared if perceptual similarity had supported relational similarity rather than conflicting with it? To achieve this support, relational similarity and perceptual similarity would have had to be correlated, which would have meant that the arrays were no longer staggered. In this situation, the object identity response and the relational response become identical, and so the predictions for the rich and the sparse stimuli should reverse. The rich stimuli should now support more relational mappings than the sparse stimuli, as the richness of their perceptual similarity is greater (with the non-staggered arrays, the child must choose the *same* object, for example, the house).

Gentner and Ratterman (1992) have shown that when the arrays in their paradigm are no longer staggered, then children's performance is indeed better with the rich stimuli than with the sparse stimuli. So perceptual similarity can support relational mappings. However, the relational training with the "Mommy", "Daddy" and "Baby" labels was omitted in this experiment, making a direct comparison with the results of their previous studies difficult.

Gentner's group has thus produced a number of studies that support the idea that superficial similarity will facilitate children's use of relational similarity. Ratterman et al.'s work has shown that when perceptual similarity cues conflict with relational similarity, then children's ability to use relational similarity is impeded. On the other hand, when object similarity is correlated with relational similarity, then relational mappings are correlated with the richness of the perceptual similarity. Gentner and Toupin have shown that perceptual similarity can support relational mappings between stories. So the degree of perceptual similarity between problems is another performance factor that can affect children's analogical reasoning.

### Do Children Shift from Using Perceptual Similarity to Using Relational Similarity?

Gentner has suggested that the role of perceptual similarity in analogy may also vary developmentally. She has proposed that there is a relational shift in children's analogical reasoning, with the ability to process perceptual similarity preceding the ability to process relational similarity (e.g. Gentner, 1988; Gentner & Ratterman, 1992). In solving analogies, she argues that children will first rely on correspondences between objects ("mere appearance"), and will only later shift to using relational similarities. The relational shift is thought to be knowledge-based, emerging at different times in different domains (Gentner & Ratterman, 1992), but what actually motivates the shift within a given domain has yet to be clarified.

Some of the evidence for the relational shift has already been discussed (Gentner & Toupin, 1986; Ratterman et al., 1987, in prep.). For example, Gentner and Ratterman discuss the Gentner and Toupin study as follows:

> The performance of the 6-year-olds was affected only by the transparency of the object correspondences: e.g., they could accurately re-tell the story when *squirrel* mapped onto *chipmunk*, but not when it mapped onto *moose*. The presence of a higher-order relational structure [provided by attaching morals to some of the stories to provide a causal structure for the protagonist's action] had no effect on them. In contrast, 9-year-olds were affected by both variables (p. 233).

So between the ages of 6 and 9 years, the children became able to use the relational structure provided by attaching morals to the stories. Other evidence for the relational shift comes from studies of metaphor interpretation (Gentner, 1988). Gentner has found that younger children (5-year-olds) produce attributional interpretations of metaphors, for example explaining that a cloud is like a sponge because "They're both round and fluffy", or that plant stems are like drinking straws because "both are tall and skinny". Older children (9-year-olds) and adults produce interpretations based on relational similarity. They might say that clouds and sponges are similar because both "store water and later give it back to you".

How compatible is Gentner's proposal of a relational shift with the view taken here that the recognition of relational similarity may not develop? Clearly, one interpretation of the relational shift idea is quite incompatible with this view. If Gentner is proposing that children will always initially solve analogies by matching objects, ignoring relational similarity even when they have represented the relations on which the analogy is based, then this would contradict the idea that the ability to recognise relational similarity does not develop. However, Gentner's claim that the shift is a function of knowledge makes it likely that her view is compatible with the approach taken here. If the relational shift corresponds to a shift from "no knowledge" to "knowledge", then children would only solve analogies on the basis of object similarities when they were ignorant of the relations on which the analogy was based. Object-matching would be a fall-back strategy in the absence of relational knowledge, and could in fact lead to successful analogical reasoning in cases where perceptual similarity and relational similarity were correlated.

## WHEN IS A RELATIONAL FOCUS SPONTANEOUS?

So far we have considered the various factors that affect children's analogical performance, and have argued that these factors perform two different functions: they help children to realise that an analogy is appropriate (noticing) and they help them to extract and represent the relations on which the analogy is based (enabling application). However, the facilitating effect of these performance factors raises a question of its own, which applies to analogical reasoning across the life span. Why are these factors necessary? Why do relatively few subjects in the studies that we have discussed spontaneously focus on relational structure in the absence of hints and other manipulations? It is unlikely that the problem is one of competence, as there is no sudden age-related shift in performance. An alternative possibility is that the disappointingly low spontaneous use of analogy found here (and also in studies with adults: see, for example, Gick & Holyoak, 1980, 1983) is a product of the laboratory-based paradigms designed to test it (see Brown, 1989).

In the problem analogy paradigm, children or adults are typically taught about a problem (the base) that has been specially chosen to involve unfamiliar variables, and that has been selected because it is unlikely to have been met previously. Their analogical ability is then measured by scoring transfer to a related but also unfamiliar target problem. For the experimenter, the target problem is clearly analogous to the base problem, but this is seldom true for the subjects. In fact, explicit instruction (or high perceptual similarity) is usually required to make the analogy apparent. Even then, transfer may not occur, as the analogy may depend on fragmentary knowledge that has just been acquired in an unfamiliar domain. Alternatively, the appropriate knowledge may be embedded in a particular context, so that the relations important to the analogy are not conceptually represented.

In these circumstances, it is not surprising that experimental subjects do not make many spontaneous analogies. As we saw earlier, subjects may even possess prior knowledge that overrides what they are being taught in the experiment, or that impedes their use of the correct analogy (e.g. Lamsfuss & Wilkening, 1991). However, if subjects possess prior knowledge that *supports* the analogy—if the analogy is set in a conceptual domain in which the relations relevant to the analogy have already been worked out—then according to our view the recognition of relational similarity should be spontaneous, unless performance factors intervene. In other words, if the analogy depends on knowledge that is coherent rather than fragmentary, then the use of analogy should be straightforward. As with classical analogies, young children should have no difficulty in solving problem analogies if they understand the relations on which the analogy is based. This is another way of describing the relational difficulty hypothesis, which we can call the "coherent knowledge hypothesis".

## Evidence for the Coherent Knowledge Hypothesis

One researcher who has argued for the coherent knowledge hypothesis is Brown (1986, 1989), who has pointed out that when it comes to reasoning, all knowledge is not equal. She has claimed that the use of analogy is difficult to prevent when knowledge is coherent:

> If that which is to be transferred consists of a coherent theory or a causal explanation that is understood, it is difficult to impede a flexible application of prior knowledge. It is when the application of a previously learned isolated rule or specific solution is required that observers decry a lack of transfer. (Brown, 1989, p. 370)

We have already seen an example of flexible application in Lamsfuss and Wilkening's children, who automatically applied the erroneous balance scale analogy to the problem about forces. So if the analogy is set in a conceptual domain in which the relations relevant to the analogy are already represented and coherently integrated, then the spontaneous use of analogy should be difficult to prevent. However, if children's knowledge about a domain is fragmentary or unassimilated, or is embedded in a particular context, then they are unlikely to use analogies spontaneously and apply their knowledge to new problems.

The coherent knowledge hypothesis is difficult to test with young children, however, because they still have such a lot to learn about the world. Much of their knowledge is actually quite incoherent. It is also true that as yet there is no good definition of what constitutes a coherent explanatory network, and no real criteria for deciding when one has been acquired. Because of this, the best way to test the predictions outlined above is probably to teach children knowledge that is thought to form a coherent explanatory network, such as knowledge that is organised around certain fundamental principles ("deep causal structure"), and then to examine whether they can make spontaneous analogies within this conceptual system.

Brown and her group took exactly this approach in a series of studies in which they taught 4-year-old children about biology. The biological domain has a rich causal structure, and it is also of intrinsic interest to children. Furthermore, it is a domain in which the fundamental principles begin to be delineated at a very young age. For example, Massey and Gelman (1988) have shown that the animate–inanimate distinction is one of the first to emerge in early childhood, at around 2 years of age. Carey (1985) has studied the development of biological understanding in some depth (see also Chapter 7), and has shown that even 4-year-olds can make sensible inferences about biological functions like eating, sleeping and reproduction. The biological domain thus provides a good source domain within which to teach children knowledge that they should be able to integrate into a deep causal structure that is already emerging within their conceptual systems.

To this end, Brown and Kane (1988) designed a number of biological analogies based either on animal defence mechanisms such as mimicry and camouflage, or on methods of natural pest control. The *defence mechanism* stories were about the hawkmoth caterpillar, which can turn over and reveal markings resembling a poisonous snake, the crested rat, which can mimic a skunk, and the capricorn beetle, which can open its wings to look like a wasp. The *natural pest control* stories concerned the ladybird (used by farmers to kill aphids), the manatee (a water mammal that eats underwater weeds, used to keep waterways clear for boats) and the purple martin (a bird that eats mosquitoes).

In their experiments, Brown and Kane told the children about one defence mechanism or pest control problem and its solution (the base), and then presented them with a second mimicry or pest control problem to solve (the target). For example, the problem about the aphids (solution = the ladybird) could be followed by the problem about the mosquitoes (solution = the purple martin). When telling the children the base stories, the experimenters took care to avoid the use of general terms that could provide clues to relational similarity (labels like "pest" or "enemy"), and to vary the descriptions of the common solutions (for example, instead of saying "mimic" in the mimicry stories, the terms "trick", "pretend" and "fool" were used). In addition to the information critical for the analogy, each of the six stories also contained irrelevant information about the animal's habitat and eating preferences. For example, the purple martin story included the critical information that (a) purple martins are birds that like to eat mosquitoes and (b) they will live in man-made bird houses, but separated these key facts with other pieces of information about purple martins.

Analogical transfer was assessed by asking the children questions such as "How could the gardener get rid of his mosquitoes?" As a comparison, a control group was told an irrelevant story prior to receiving the target problem, and was then asked the same questions. If children make analogies spontaneously when the analogies are based on a coherent system of knowledge, and have successfully integrated the new knowledge about mimicry and pest control with their existing biological knowledge, then the children in the analogy group should be more likely to solve the target problem correctly than the children in the control group. This was exactly what Brown and Kane found. The children who had received the base analogy were highly successful at solving the target problem (approximately 80% solved the target correctly), whereas the children in the control group were not (approximately 10% solved the target correctly). One of Brown's favourite examples of successful analogical reasoning comes from Jeremy, who considered how the gardener could get rid of his mosquitoes and said, "... well, he could build a house for these purple martins at the bottom of the garden ... but I think Raid [an insect spray] is best—but it's just like the others we talked about, like the ladybugs eating the farmer's bugs—we talked about this" (p. 510).

So the 4-year-olds in Brown and Kane's study were able to focus on relational structure spontaneously, without the support of any of the performance factors that we discussed earlier. They used analogies even though the perceptual similarity between the biological examples (e.g.

a bird and a ladybug) was fairly low, no hints to use analogy were given, they received only one prior example of an analogous solution, and they were not being instructed to reflect on their solutions in any way. Although the children were again taught the information necessary to the analogies at the time of the experiment (e.g. the mimicry information), they were apparently successful in this case because they already had a network of knowledge about animals and their survival into which this new knowledge could be integrated. Their knowledge was already structured in a way that enabled analogies. This seems to be persuasive evidence for the claim that when the basis for analogy is a coherent conceptual system in which the important relations are already represented, then transfer is difficult to impede.

Another way of testing the coherent knowledge hypothesis is to study younger children. In the learning set experiments discussed earlier in this chapter, 3-year-olds seemed unable to display the levels of spontaneous transfer achieved by the 4- and 5-year-olds. The learning set paradigm (A1–A2, B1–B2, C1–C2) required the children to form an abstract rule to look for analogies (a learning set) as well as to extract the particular analogous relation in each problem pair. One explanation of the 3-year-olds' poor performance in this paradigm is that they may have been being asked to solve analogies that were based on knowledge that was, for them, fragmentary and incoherent. If this were the case, then their performance levels in the learning set paradigm should improve if they are asked to make analogies that are based on a coherent system of knowledge instead.

Either of these requirements could have caused difficulties for the 3-year-olds in Brown et al.'s earlier studies. If their failure was based on an inability to extract the analogous relations, however, then the use of a coherent knowledge domain should solve this problem. When knowledge is coherent, then even 3-year-olds should be able to extract the appropriate relations. It should thus be possible to measure the ability of this age group to form a learning set separately from their ability to extract relations.

To test this prediction, Brown and Kane designed pairs of problems that were set in a domain with deep causal structure, namely biology. Three pairs of biological stories were used, based on the animal defence mechanisms of *camouflage by colour change* (the arctic fox, which undergoes a seasonal colour change, and the chameleon, which fluctuates in colour); *camouflage by shape change* (the walking stick insect, which can resemble a twig or leaf, and the pipe fish, which can resemble a reed); and *mimicry* (the crested rat, which can resemble a skunk, and the hawkmoth caterpillar, which can resemble a poisonous snake). Transfer was tested by asking the children questions about defence, such as "How could the hawkmoth caterpillar stop the big bird that wants to eat him?" (the answer is to look like a snake). As previously, the measure of learning set was performance on the final problem in the third problem pair (C2).

In the earlier learning set study based on the relations of *swinging*, *stacking* and *pulling*, the 3-year-olds had shown only 40% successful transfer in the third problem pair. With the biological analogies, they showed 70–80% successful analogical transfer on the third problem (C2), thereby doubling their previous success rate. For example, 3-year-old Aaron was able to reason that the hawkmoth caterpillar, which can look like a poisonous snake to deter predators, and the porcupine fish, which can double its size and raise spikes to deter predators, had evolved analogous solutions to the problem of avoiding predation. The experimenter asked him whether they were the same kind of stories. He replied "Yes, they are the same. ... Both of them have a mean guy that wants to eat them all up. ... When the bird wants to eat him [pointing to the caterpillar] he gets really mean and changes himself into a snake ... this one [pointing to the porcupine fish] can look mean too! He gets mean and big and gets all his scary pointers [spikes] out. ... They both get mean and scary so they [the predators] run away!" The experimenter commented "They're pretty smart, huh?", and Aaron agreed "Just like me!" (Brown, 1989).

Furthermore, Brown reports that the 3-year-olds maintained these high reasoning levels in the absence of instructions to reflect on their solutions, and without support from any other performance factors such as perceptual similarity. This is very strong evidence for the coherent knowledge claim. Brown has shown that when analogies are set in a domain with a deep causal structure that children have already begun to represent, then even 3-year-olds can spontaneously form a learning set to look for analogies, and furthermore that they can do so even when they have only just learned about the particular animal examples involved.

## Summary

In general, therefore, research with problem analogies has supported the conclusions that emerged from our survey of research with classical analogies. Evidence from both paradigms has demonstrated that the ability to reason about relational similarity is present very early in development, as long as the children have the relevant relational knowledge. In addition, evidence from the problem analogy paradigm has shown that children's ability to use relational similarity will vary with certain performance factors. These factors can determine whether the analogy is noticed, and how easy it is to apply.

Research in the problem analogy paradigm has also confirmed that all knowledge is not equal. When knowledge is fragmentary, or is embedded in a particular context, then it is difficult for children to recognise or to extract the relations on which the analogy is based. This finding poses a general theoretical problem for a knowledge-based view of analogy, a problem which was also raised in relation to classical analogies. The problem is how the researcher (or teacher) can decide whether knowledge is fragmentary or contextually embedded independently of failure or success on the analogy task itself. How can one assess the degree of a child's relational knowledge independently of that child's failure to reason by analogy?

One solution to this problem is to take a relational domain that is already fairly well worked-out, and then to set either classical or problem analogies within that domain, taking care to include a control condition to check that the children do have the relational knowledge that is being attributed to them. Independent measures of a child's relational knowledge have been used in classical analogy tasks (e.g. Goswami & Brown, 1989), but not with problem analogies. Alternatively, children can be taught the requisite relational knowledge prior to presenting them with the analogies. This solution has been used in problem analogy tasks (e.g. Brown & Kane, 1988), but not with classical analogies. Research using both of these approaches has established that when children understand the relations in an analogy, then they can reason about relational similarity at ages as young as 3 years.

What about even younger children? According to the extreme version of the knowledge-based view of analogical reasoning being proposed here, the ability to use relational similarity may not develop at all. This view would predict that children should be sensitive to relational similarity from very early in life, perhaps even from infancy. To test this prediction, we need evidence about analogical reasoning in babies. As we will see in the next chapter, there are some intriguing findings with infants that suggest that they, too, are sensitive to relational similarity.

CHAPTER SIX

# Analogies in Babies and Toddlers

The argument pursued so far in this book has been that the ability to apply the relational similarity constraint may not develop. What seems to develop instead is the knowledge base to which this constraint is applied. As the child's knowledge about the world grows, so the structure of this knowledge will change, and the awareness of different relationships within a given domain will increase, enabling deeper or more complex analogies.

All the experimental work that we have considered so far has been based on one kind of knowledge, namely *conceptual* knowledge. The relational difficulty hypothesis has an obvious role to play in explaining such analogies, as a clear understanding of the relationships within a given conceptual field is required if the child is to make analogies within that field. Brown's work with biological analogies provided a simple example of this. The children in her studies could not have made analogies about animal defence mechanisms or natural pest control without some knowledge about the relationships that held within the biological domain.

In this chapter, I will look at experiments that can tell us something about the roots of this relational competence, which means looking at empirical work with young infants. Experiments with infants tend to be based on perceptual rather than conceptual comparisons, however, and the idea of relational difficulty is less clear-cut if we are considering perceptual knowledge. On the one hand, it can be argued that perceptual relationships are imposed on the stimuli by the beholder. As adults, we may describe a tone of music as ascending, and hence as relationally similar to an arrow depicting the direction "upwards", but the common relationship of "ascending" is a feature of our mental representation of these physical events. On the other hand, it can be argued that perceptual events are inherently structured, and that we as adults recognise a relational similarity between ascending tones and visual symbols specifying ascent because of this structural similarity. There may be acoustic properties of tones (such as timbre) that convey direction, and visual properties of arrows (such as the locus of highest density) that also convey direction. So the similarity between an "up" arrow and an ascending tone may be recognisable at a perceptual level, on the basis of inherent properties of the stimuli.

The recognition of a similarity between stimuli such as an ascending tone and an "up" arrow may be an early form of analogical comparison. In this chapter, I have selected some experiments with infants that show that babies, too, can recognise structural similarity. Unfortunately, such experiments are rather thin on the ground. However, they are worth considering because it can be argued that the recognition of structural similarities between perceptual stimuli, which adults would represent as relational similarities, provide us with evidence about the roots of relational competence (see also Marks, Hammeal & Bornstein, 1987, who have argued that children and adults perceive perceptual properties such as loudness and brightness as being similar, and that this might be a precursor of metaphorical reasoning). More controversial examples of relational comparisons, such as experiments on cross-modal matching, will be omitted from this discussion.

## EVIDENCE FOR SENSITIVITY TO RELATIONAL SIMILARITY IN INFANTS

Most of the research concerning the understanding of relational similarity in infants is based on a paradigm called habituation. In habituation studies, infants are first exposed to one stimulus, the habituating stimulus, until their interest in it wanes (usually measured by a decrease in looking time). They are then presented with a new stimulus, the dishabituating stimulus, which is unfamiliar. The looking time that they devote to this new stimulus is then measured. If they show interest in the new stimulus (a significant increase in looking time), then it is assumed that they can discriminate the new stimulus from the previous one. Variations on the habituation technique include presenting a pair of stimuli (e.g. familiar and unfamiliar) at the test phase to see which is preferred, or simply measuring a looking preference between two stimuli without prior exposure to a habituating stimulus.

## "Metaphorical Matching"

Perhaps the most ingenious investigation of infants' sensitivity to relational similarity concerned their ability to perform matches between stimuli such as ascending tones and arrows pointing in an upwards direction (Wagner, Winner, Cicchetti & Gardner, 1981). These so-called "metaphorical" matches depended on the recognition of the similarity of relations such as continuity/discontinuity, or ascending/descending, between both a visual and an auditory stimulus. For example, in the case of the arrow, the infants were shown two visual stimuli, an arrow pointing upwards and an arrow pointing downwards. They were then played either an ascending tone or a descending tone. Wagner et al.'s question was whether the infants would show a visual preference for the "up" arrow in the presence of the ascending tone, and a preference for the "down" arrow in the presence of the descending tone. They argued that such visual preferences would indicate that the infants were matching the stimuli on the basis of relations like "ascending".

Other metaphorical matches used by Wagner et al. included a broken line and a pulsing tone *vs* a continuous line and a smooth tone, and a jagged circle and a pulsing tone *vs* a smooth circle and a continuous tone. They argued that none of these auditory–visual matches could be made on the basis of physical similarity (e.g. increasing intensity of both the auditory and the visual stimuli). They also noted that it was unlikely that infants would have had prior experience of these co-occurrences. So any preferential matching that did occur should be due to the recognition of similarity at a more abstract relational level.

In fact, Wagner et al. found preferential "metaphorical" matching for all of the examples described above. Infants as young as 9 months of age preferred to look at the "up" arrow rather than at the "down" arrow when they heard a tone that was ascending, and at the "down" arrow rather than at the "up" arrow when the tone was descending. They preferred the broken line when the tone was pulsing, and the continuous line when the tone was continuous. This is a remarkable result. It suggests that the infants were responding on the basis of relational similarity. These early analogies suggest that certain relational correspondences can be recognised very early in development.

## Research on Number

Further evidence for the recognition of relational similarity in infancy can be found in research on the perception of number. Changes in numerosity can be described in terms of relations such as "greater than" and "less than", and experiments can investigate infants' recognition of such changes in relative numerosity across different arrays. For example, if habituation is to a series of arrays representing the relation "greater than", and at dishabituation the infants are shown a new array representing the relation "less than", a novelty response can be interpreted as showing that the infants are sensitive to relational similarity. Dishabituation would be based on the recognition of a change in the similarity of the *relationship* between the arrays.

Cooper (1984) has reported a series of experiments based on this technique. In his studies, infants were required to detect changes in the relationships between numbers of coloured squares. The infants were shown pairs of displays of these squares, which either represented the "greater than" relationship, the "less than" relationship or an "equal to" relationship. For example, for the "greater than" relationship the series of pairs might be 4:2, 4:3 and 2:1, while for the "less than" relationship they might be 3:4, 2:4 and 1:2. The squares in each pair differed in size and in spatial arrangement between the first and the second arrays, and also from trial to trial. An example is shown in Table 6.1.

At test, the infants were shown either (1) a reversed relationship (3:4 for the "greater than" example), (2) an "equal" relationship (2:2) or (3) a novel example of the same relationship (3:2). If infants are sensitive to relational similarity, then they should show dishabituation in the first two of these conditions, but not in the third. Cooper found that infants aged 10–12 months dishabituated to equality only, suggesting that their relational discrimination was limited to the differentiation of equality from inequality. Infants aged 14–16 months dishabituated both to the "equal" relationship and to the reversal ("less than"), indicating that they were also aware of whether the relative numerosity of the displays had changed direction (from "greater than" to "less than"). So at both ages, the infants were able to detect similarities in the *relations* between the numerosity of the pairs of stimuli, shown by habituation, and to respond to changes in these relations, shown by dishabituation. Thus even at 10 months of age, infants seem to be sensitive to similarities in relative numerosity.

## Social Mirroring

A third source of data on infants' recognition of relational similarity comes from research on infant imitation. In some recent work extending his classic imitation studies (e.g. Meltzoff & Moore, 1977, 1983), Meltzoff has investigated whether infants can recognise when adults are imitating *them* (Meltzoff, 1990). Meltzoff has argued that recognising that someone else is imitating *you* implies a recognition of the structural equivalence between another agent's behaviour and your own: You

TABLE 6.1

Examples of the Numerosity Arrays used by Cooper (1984)[a]

| Condition | Numerosity of Array 1 | Numerosity of Array 2 | Trial Type |
|---|---|---|---|
| Less than | | | |
| Habituation | 3 | 4 | |
| | 2 | 4 | |
| | 1 | 2 | |
| Test | 3 | 4 | Old |
| | 2 | 3 | New |
| | 4 | 3 | Reversed |
| | 2 | 2 | Equal |
| Greater than | | | |
| Habituation | 4 | 2 | |
| | 4 | 3 | |
| | 2 | 1 | |
| Test | 4 | 3 | Old |
| | 3 | 2 | New |
| | 3 | 4 | Reversed |
| | 2 | 2 | Equal |
| Equal | | | |
| Habituation | 4 | 4 | |
| | 2 | 2 | |
| | 1 | 1 | |
| Test | 4 | 4 | Old |
| | 3 | 3 | New |
| | 2 | 4 | Less than |
| | 4 | 2 | Greater than |

[a] Reproduced with permission

realise that whatever you do, they will do likewise. In contrast, imitating a gesture made by someone else only implies a detection of the similarity between two actions at a behavioural level.

In these "social mirroring" studies, the infant was actually copied by *two* adult experimenters. One of them copied the infant's current behaviour with a toy, and the other copied a behaviour that the infant had produced at an earlier time. The behaviour of both experimenters was yoked, and depended on a predetermined schedule pairing certain actions, such as "shake" and "slide". For example, if the baby was currently shaking his toy, the first experimenter would shadow the infant and also shake his toy, while the second experimenter would slide his toy. If the baby changed to sliding his toy, the first experimenter would start sliding his toy, while the second experimenter would change to shaking his toy. This technique equated the temporal equivalence of the actions of the baby and of the experimenters, and also their contingency, but meant that only one of the experimenter's actions was structurally equivalent to the action of the baby. If the baby did not produce one of the pre-scheduled behaviours, both experimenters sat passively.

Meltzoff found that the infants (14-month-olds) preferred to watch and smile at the adult who was imitating their current behaviour rather than their past behaviour. He argued that this preference must have been based on the structural equivalence (or relational similarity) between the infants' own actions and those of the imitating experimenter. The possibility that the infants were responding on the basis of common movement (e.g. a looking preference for "shaking") was ruled out by evidence that the babies actively tested a "copying hypothesis" during the experiment. For example, they would shake their own toy faster and faster, and then suddenly stop, to see whether the first experimenter would follow suit. Significantly more of this hypothesis-testing behaviour was directed towards the imitating experimenter than towards the yoked experimenter. So the babies did seem to be responding on the basis of the relational similarity between their actions and those of the imitating experimenter.

Research on social mirroring, on early numerosity and on metaphorical matching has thus provided a variety of evidence that infants are sensitive to relational similarites in the perceptual realm. So the basic requirement for an analogical capacity—the recognition of relational similarity—is present very early in development. We turn now to experiments that investigate whether infants can also *use* relational similarities to make inferences about perceptual events. Recent research by Baillargeon and her colleagues on the development of infants' understanding of the physical world has suggested that infants will frequently use relational comparisons to make predictions about events in the physical realm.

## EVIDENCE FOR THE USE OF RELATIONAL COMPARISONS BY INFANTS

Infants' use of relational comparisons can be illustrated by the inferences that they make about at least three classes of physical events. The three classes that will be discussed are predicting the size of hidden objects, predicting the point at which moving objects will stop when they encounter barriers, and predicting the degree of displacement of stationary objects when they are hit by moving objects. For all three classes of physical event, Baillargeon has evidence that infants will use relational similarities to make inferences about the behaviour of the objects involved.

## The Size of Hidden Objects

For example, consider the development of the understanding that an object hidden under a cloth will cause a lump in that cloth. How might infants infer the size of the hidden object from the size of the lump? Baillargeon (in press) has suggested that the infants will have at least two strategies available to them, a *quantitative* strategy and a *qualitative* strategy. The first involves estimating the approximate size of the lump, and then using this to estimate the approximate size of the object that should emerge from beneath the cloth. This inference depends on an estimation of *absolute* quantity. The second strategy involves comparing the size of the lump to the size of the object that emerges by using a reference point to remember the size of the lump. This inference involves a *relational* comparison (i.e. that the relation between lump A and reference point B is the same as the relation between object C and reference point B).

Interestingly, Baillargeon (1991) and Baillargeon and DeVos (1991) have shown that infants will use qualitative strategies in making inferences about the size of hidden objects before they will use quantitative ones. In their experiments, infants were first shown a cloth with a protuberance beneath it. As the infant watched, a screen was raised in front of the cloth, and a hand reached behind the screen. The hand then reappeared holding either a small toy dog of the same size as the protuberance (a *possible* hidden object), or a large toy dog that was much bigger than the protuberance (an *impossible* hidden object). In one condition, a second cloth with an identical protuberance remained visible as a reference point. In a second condition, there was no reference point. The experimental condition is shown in Fig. 6.1.

If infants can make absolute judgements about quantity, then they should be surprised at the emergence of the impossibly large dog in both of these conditions. However, if they initially rely on a relational comparison to estimate the size of the object beneath the lump, then they should only be surprised at the emergence of the large dog in the first condition, and not in the second. This was exactly the result that Baillargeon and DeVos found. The infants (aged 12½ months) only looked significantly longer at the emergence of the impossible object in the first condition, when they could use a relational comparison to estimate the size of the hidden object. They did not show surprise at the emergence of the large dog in the second condition until later in development (13½ months). So the ability to use relational comparisons may actually emerge first developmentally, before the ability to make absolute estimates of quantity. Baillargeon's proposed

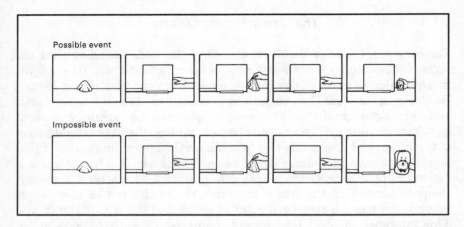

FIG. 6.1. The experimental condition in the "Lump Task" (reproduced with permission from Baillargeon & DeVos, 1991).

developmental sequence would make sense, as it may be cognitively simpler to make a relational comparison than to remember an absolute quantity (see also Bryant, 1974).

## Encountering a Hidden Barrier

Evidence that infants will use relational comparisons before making absolute judgements is not restricted to experiments about judging size. Baillargeon has also shown that relational comparisons are used in judging the point at which a moving object should stop when it encounters a barrier. In her experiments, the barrier is actually obscured from view by the movement of the object, and so the stopping point must either be estimated by using a reference point (qualitatively) or by remembering the absolute location and size of the hidden barrier (quantitatively).

To investigate which of these strategies the infants used first, Baillargeon designed a series of experiments using a rotating screen (e.g. Baillargeon, 1987, in press; Baillargeon, Spelke & Wasserman, 1985). In these experiments, the infants were initially habituated to the movement of the screen through an arc of 180° (it moved back and forth, like a drawbridge). They were then shown two events, a *possible* event and an *impossible* event. In the possible event, a box was placed behind the screen, and the screen accordingly stopped rotating at the point at which it came into contact with the box (by which time the box was hidden from the infants' view by the screen). In the impossible event, the screen continued along its path, apparently moving through the solid box. For half of the infants, this violation was extreme—the screen apparently moved through the top 80% of the box before coming to rest. For the other half, the violation was more moderate—the screen apparently moved through the top 50% of the box before stopping. This experimental paradigm is depicted in Fig. 6.2.

Baillargeon found that infants as young as 4½ months of age could detect these violations if (and only if) they could use a relational comparison. If a second, identical box was placed to the right of the first box, in the same fronto-parallel plane, but out of the path of the screen, then the infants could work out where the screen should stop, and they could detect both of the violations (80% and 50%). If the second box was not present, or if it was not in the same fronto-parallel plane as the first box, then they were unable to detect either violation. Interestingly, however, if the second box was too dissimilar in appearance from the first—if, for example, it was yellow and was decorated with a clown's face, whereas the first box was red and was decorated with white dots—

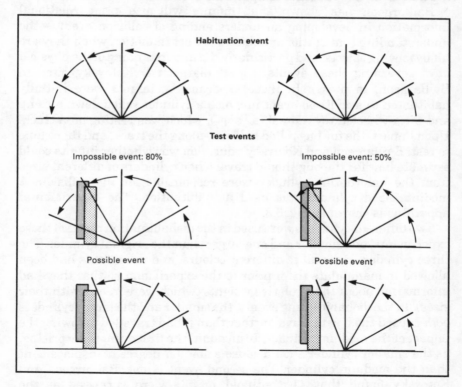

FIG. 6.2. The Rotating Screen Task (Baillargeon, 1987. Copyright 1987 by the American Psychological Association. Reprinted by permission.).

then the infants ceased to use the box as a basis for making a relational comparison. So infants benefit from perceptual similarity when they are making inferences about relational similarity, just as older children and adults do.

## Collision Events

All of the relational comparisons that we have been considering so far have depended on the use of reference points that were physically present. In these experiments, the information necessary for the relational comparisons was perceptually available to the infants at the time that they needed it. However, Baillargeon also has evidence that infants can use *prior* relational information to understand physical events. This is a particularly interesting result with respect to our question about the use of relational similarity, as it shows that infants are able to make relational comparisons over time.

Baillargeon has shown that infants will use prior relational information in developing an understanding of collision events—the understanding that stationary objects are set in motion when they are hit by moving objects, and particularly the understanding of the physical laws governing these events (e.g. Baillargeon & Kotovsky, cited in Baillargeon, in press). In these experiments, infants were initially habituated to a collision event in which a cylinder rolled down a ramp and hit a wheeled toy animal (a "bug"), which was resting on a track. Upon impact, the toy bug rolled half-way along the track, and then came to rest. Baillargeon and Kotovsky's question was whether infants could estimate how far the bug should travel when cylinders of different sizes from the habituating cylinder were responsible for the collision. A medium-sized cylinder was used at habituation. The experimental apparatus is shown in Fig. 6.3.

Two different cylinders were used in the dishabituation phase of these experiments, one smaller and one larger than the original cylinder. The three cylinders were all of different colours, and the infants had been allowed to manipulate them prior to the experiment, so that they had information about their relative weights (which were in line with their sizes). In the dishabituating events, the smaller and the larger cylinders *both* caused the bug to travel farther than it had travelled following the impact of the medium cylinder. To an adult, the first event is surprising, as the smaller cylinder should cause a smaller degree of displacement than the medium cylinder. The second event is not. Baillargeon and Kotovsky found that 11-month-old infants were surprised at the outcome of the small cylinder event, but not at the outcome of the large cylinder event.

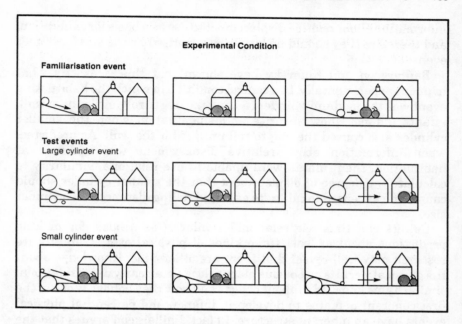

FIG. 6.3. The "Bug" Task: Medium cylinder habituating event (reproduced with permission from Baillargeon, in press).

This result implies that the infants were able to make relational comparisons over time. They inferred that if a medium cylinder caused a medium displacement of the bug, then a smaller cylinder should cause a smaller displacement of the bug, and a larger cylinder should cause a larger displacement. This meant that they were surprised when the smaller cylinder caused the bug to roll to the end of the track, but not when the larger cylinder did so. Baillargeon argues that this is evidence that the infants were *calibrating* their predictions about the physical events, reasoning that the bug should travel farther with the large than with the medium cylinder, and farther with the medium than with the small cylinder.

Although such behaviour may seem unexpectedly sophisticated for young infants, it is simple to test whether such calibration was taking place. The test is to withhold information about the relative distance of displacement during the habituation phase of the experiment. If the medium cylinder causes the bug to travel to the end of the track at habituation, then there is no reason to expect the smaller cylinder to cause relatively less displacement in the dishabituation phase, as the bug might have been able to travel much further at habituation if the track had been longer. In this case, the infants would have no information about *relative* displacement to use as a basis for calibration, and therefore they should no longer be surprised by the small cylinder event.

Baillargeon and Kotovsky have shown that this is exactly what happens experimentally. In a control condition in which the habituating event was the medium cylinder causing the bug to roll until it hit a wall, infants did not show surprise at dishabituation when the smaller cylinder also caused the bug to roll until it hit the wall. As predicted, when information about relative displacement was withheld at habituation, then infants were unable to use relational similarity to calculate the degree of displacement that the smaller cylinder should cause, and so ceased to calibrate expected rolling distance with cylinder size.

Infants can thus use relational similarity as a basis for making predictions about at least three kinds of physical events, and future research may well reveal that there are others, too. Knowledge about the physical world is an obvious place to look for an early use of relational similarity, as knowledge about objects and how they behave is one of the first coherent domains to develop in infancy, and perceptual physical events have an inherent structure. In fact, Baillargeon argues that the infants in her studies were *reasoning* about the physical world, as their inferences were based on representations of the physical events. In other work, she has shown that infants can make predictions about information that is perceptually hidden, and so must be mentally represented. These results imply that the infants' knowledge about physical events is conceptual as well as perceptual, and Mandler (1992) has proposed a theory about how perceptual relational structures may develop into conceptual ones that is partly based on Baillargeon's work.

## EVIDENCE FOR SENSITIVITY TO RELATIONAL SIMILARITY IN TODDLERS

Studies with very young infants have mainly relied on looking time as a measure of the recognition of relational similarity. Once infants become able to act on their environments and to move around, however, then it becomes possible to use paradigms closer to traditional problem-solving analogies to examine their recognition and use of relational similarity. We will look at two sets of studies that have used a problem-solving paradigm to examine analogies in slightly older children (1- and 2-year-olds). One set of studies is based on tool-use and the other is based on search.

## Tool-use Studies

Tool-use provides a relatively straightforward means of studying children's understanding of relational similarity. If children are taught that problem A can be solved with tool B, and are then given a new problem C which is similar to problem A, we can ask whether they will select a tool D that is similar to tool B to solve problem C. This was essentially the technique used by Holyoak et al. in their genie paradigm.

Brown (1989, 1990) used this technique with 1- and 2-year-olds. She asked them to solve some "pulling" problems in which they had to use different tools to gain access to toys such as Mickey Mouse. The toys were placed just out of reach, and a variety of tools were provided for pulling them closer, including a long stick, a long hook, a long cane and a long rake. All of the tools were painted with red and white stripes to make them look similar, but only some of them were actually useful for reaching the toy (e.g. the hook). Brown's question was whether the children would use relational similarity to decide which tools could and could not give them access to the toys across different trials. Examples of the different tools that she used are shown in Fig. 6.4.

The children first learned to solve one example of this "pulling problem", either alone or with their mother's help (79% of those under 24 months needed help). They were then given a transfer task using a new set of tools, most of which could not be used to reach the toy (e.g. a long stick, a "swizzle stick"). One of the transfer tools was always perceptually similar to the tools in the learning set (it was candy-striped), but this tool was the *wrong* solution to the pulling problem (e.g. it had no pulling head). One tool was relationally similar to the correct tool in the learning set, and this tool was perceptually dissimilar to the previous solution (e.g. a black rake). Children's preferred tool in the transfer task was nearly always the relationally-similar tool: 92% chose the tool that enabled pulling (defined as one that was rigid, of sufficient length and with an effective pulling head).

Brown argues that this is a genuine example of relational transfer. Although she did not measure whether the children would have chosen the appropriate tool (e.g. the black rake) without prior experience of the base problem, she points out that other aspects of her study suggest that experience of the pulling solution with the hook was necessary for transfer to the target problem with the rake. The youngest children (17–24 months) needed their mothers to demonstrate the pulling solution before they could successfully reach for the toy in the base problem, and so it is unlikely that they would have selected the black rake if this had been presented on the first trial. Furthermore, the children did not reject tools that were too flexible, too short or that had no effective pulling

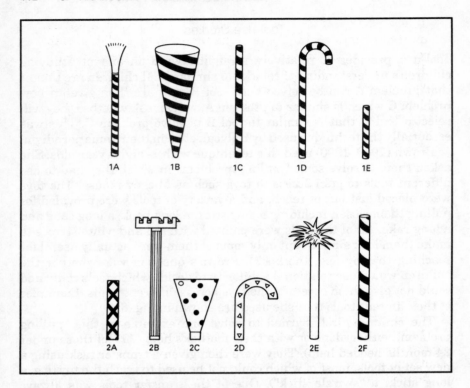

FIG. 6.4. The learning and transfer tools in the Reaching Task (reproduced with permission from Brown, 1989).

head in the learning phase of the experiment, but they consistently rejected such tools in the transfer phase. Brown argues that this discerning transfer behaviour must have been based on the relation "enables pulling", as this was the only similarity between the preferred tools.

## Search Tasks

Search tasks can also provide a way of studying the use of relational similarity by very young children. In Chapter 5 we saw that Ratterman et al. (1987, in prep.) used a "find-the-sticker" task based on relational size to examine relational mappings in searching behaviour. Deloache has also developed a different search task for studying children's understanding of relational similarity, based on scale models.

In her task, 2- to 3-year-old children are asked to find toys concealed in a room in her laboratory by using a scale model (Deloache, 1987, 1989,

1990). The model room is a perfect replica of the real room. It is the same colour, it has windows and doors in the same places, and it has replicas of the same pieces of furniture in the same locations (see Fig. 6.5). The children's job is to find a Snoopy toy hidden in the real room after being shown where a tiny model Snoopy is hiding in the model room. They are told explicitly that the model room can help them to solve this problem, as both "Little Snoopy" and "Big Snoopy" like to hide in the same places. The question is whether they can understand that Little Snoopy's hiding place in the model room can provide them with the information necessary to locate Big Snoopy in the real room.

In her studies, Deloache finds a dramatic and sudden developmental shift in children's ability to use the relational correspondences between the real room and the model. Thirty-month-olds are very poor at using the hiding place in the model room to guide their search, even though they can remember where Little Snoopy is hiding, whereas 36-month-olds effortlessly retrieve Big Snoopy from the correct location in the real room. Deloache identifies the failure of the 30-month-olds as a failure of "representational insight". She argues that to succeed in her task, the children have to understand both the relational correspondences between the real room and the model room, and what it is to "represent" something. If children do not understand much about representation, then they might think that the model is a toy in its own right, and so might be unable to disembed the representational capacity of the model from its function as a toy. They lack the "representational insight" to understand that it actually represents the real room. This lack of insight prevents them from representing and using the relational correspondences between the model and the room, correspondences that are crystal-clear to the older children.

If the "representational insight" explanation is correct, then the 30-month-olds should be able to recognise the relational correspondences between the model and the room if they can be made aware of the representational relationship between them. To test this prediction, however, we need to devise a way of giving younger children representational insight. Deloache's solution to this transfer problem has been to use photographs.

Photographs, in contrast to models, are purely representational media. Their sole function is to depict objects, locations and people in the real world. Deloache reasoned that if she used photographs to show the children where Little Snoopy was hiding, then the search task would become one of simply using the relational similarities between the photographs and the room to locate Big Snoopy. The "representational insight" requirement inherent in the model task would be removed.

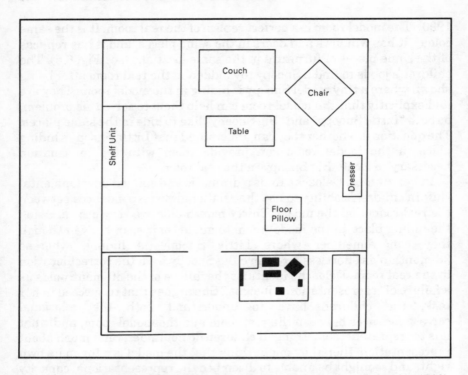

FIG. 6.5. The Scale Model Task (reproduced with permission from Deloache, 1989).

The photographs that Deloache decided to use either depicted the whole room in her laboratory, or depicted single pieces of furniture in that room (she has also used paper-and-pencil sketches, which work just as well). The children were either shown where Little Snoopy was hiding by the experimenter pointing to the hiding location in the photographs, or by actually depicting Little Snoopy partially concealed in his hiding place. As Deloache predicted, once the "representational insight" requirement of the model task was removed, the 30-month-olds had no difficulty in finding Big Snoopy. They also showed successful transfer from the photographs to the model, and even to a search task using maps. The transfer data are particularly important, as they imply that the stumbling block in the model task really was one of representational insight. So children can use relational correspondences to search successfully for objects. The connection between analogy and the understanding of representation and symbolism is a fascinating one, and has hardly begun to be studied (see Haskell, 1989).

## Summary

The research reviewed in this chapter has shown that relational similarity is recognised and used by both infants and toddlers. Infants can appreciate that an arrow pointing upwards and an ascending tone are similar (Wagner et al., 1981), can recognise similarities between relative numerosity (Cooper, 1984) and can recognise structural correspondences between their own behaviour and that of another person (Meltzoff, 1990). They can also use relational comparisons as a basis for making inferences about physical events (e.g. Baillargeon, in press), and a few months later, become able to appreciate and use relational similarities in problem-solving tasks requiring the appropriate use of tools and the location of hidden objects.

Having discussed evidence that the ability to recognise and use relational similarity is present very early in development, we turn finally to a consideration of children's spontaneous use of analogy in learning. In the next chapter, we will consider children's use of analogies in the "real worlds" of their classrooms.

# CHAPTER SEVEN

# Analogies in the Real World of the Classroom

It is time to assess what we know about children's understanding of analogy. A number of themes have emerged from the research discussed in this book.

## COMMON THEMES

### Relational Knowledge

One important theme has been that children will fail analogy tasks if they do not understand the relations on which an analogy is based. This conclusion has emerged from both of the major research paradigms used to study analogy. Classical analogy studies have shown that there is a significant link between relational difficulty and analogical success. Problem analogy studies have found that it is often necessary to help children to reflect on relational knowledge that they already possess in an embedded form in order to help them to reason successfully by analogy.

The importance of relational knowledge to successful analogising may also explain why analogies are a good correlate of I.Q. Children with a deeper conceptual understanding of a given domain will have represented more of the relationships that hold within that domain, and thus will be able to solve more complex analogies set within the domain. This idea is supported by information-processing research, which has shown that the components of inference (working out the relation that links the A and the B terms in a classical analogy) and application (applying an analogous relation to the C term) are important in analogical success. Both of these components depend on relational knowledge. So the underlying message from all these lines of research has been the same: Children will not be able to reason by analogy if they are ignorant of the relations on which the analogy is based.

## Not All Knowlege is Equal

The second theme that has emerged from the research discussed in this book is that not all knowledge is equal. Simply teaching children the relations relevant to a particular analogy in a piecemeal fashion will not necessarily result in successful analogical performance. The relations might be meaningless in the absence of other knowledge that supports the new knowledge or that makes it coherent. For example, 3-year-olds showed greater success in using analogies based on integrated biological knowledge than in using analogies based on arbitrary relations between physical actions (such as stacking tyres and bales of hay: Brown & Kane, 1988). So analogies are easier to use when the relational knowledge on which they are based is part of a coherent system of conceptual knowledge, such as a causal explanatory network.

## Inducing Analogy

Thirdly, we now have quite a good understanding of how to encourage the use of analogy when it is not used spontaneously. Children can be induced to recognise the relational similarity between analogous problems either by the experimenter simply telling them that the problems are the same (or providing hints), or by the experimenter presenting them with multiple examples of analogy (enabling the formation of a "general solution schema", or a "learning set" to look for analogy). Children can also be helped to focus on relations by being asked to reflect on their learning, for example by having to teach someone else to solve the same problems (e.g. a Kermit puppet), or by describing how the problems are the same to the experimenter. Finally, children can be helped to extract the relational structure of the base problem in story-mapping tasks by questioning them about the goal structure of the story. All of these manipulations have the same effect: They encourage children to represent explicitly the relational structure of the problem, so that they can go on to make an analogy.

## Predictions

We can now make two predictions about how analogy should operate in the real world outside the psychological laboratory, when it is used to acquire knowledge. Firstly, analogy should be used spontaneously when the knowledge that it depends on is part of a coherent and well-understood domain. In these circumstances, and if performance factors do not intervene, analogical reasoning should be fast and automatic. Analogies should be made without the child needing to be told that an analogy is appropriate, and in the absence of hints or instructions designed to aid the extraction of the relations on which the analogy is based.

Secondly, in circumstances in which the child needs to think about using an analogy (as in many of the experiments that we have considered in this book), it is crucial that the relations on which the analogies depend should be familiar ones. Children cannot reason by analogy about relations that they do not understand. So if analogies are to be used successfully in the classroom, then they should be based on relations that are already well-known, and the analogy should be made explicit to the children as well. To reason by analogy, they may need a number of examples of analogous problems and their solutions, or they may need help in extracting the relations from the context in which they have been learned. So as well as providing a variety of examples, it may be necessary to instruct children about the analogies themselves if the goal is intellectual development.

I will discuss three areas of classroom research that are relevant to these predictions: biology, reading and mathematics. Children's use of analogy in biology and in reading provide examples of the spontaneous use of analogy. Young children extend their biological knowledge by making analogies based on people, and make analogies to read new words once they have acquired a particular kind of knowledge about spoken language. As they read, children also use analogies to help in the acquisition and comprehension of new information in their textbooks. Children can be taught to apply certain strategies to help them to comprehend text, and will go on to learn new information by analogy while practising these strategies. So the use of analogies in text comprehension will be considered as well.

Secondly, we will consider the use of analogies in teaching mathematics. Analogies are a popular way of teaching children mathematical concepts, even though the children are often very poor at using the analogies that their teachers devise. This failure can be explained in terms of the number and kind of analogical examples that they are given, and the method and timing of their presentation. Teachers often assume that giving the children the right analogy will be sufficient for learning. Transfer from the analogical base to the target mathematical concept is expected to be automatic. Because of this assumption, the teachers rarely instruct the children about the analogies themselves. To the teachers, the analogies are so transparent that they do not require explanation. However, to the children, the analogies may not be obvious at all.

# THE SPONTANEOUS USE OF ANALOGY

## Analogies in Biology

Studies of children's developing biological knowledge have shown that young children will make decisions about whether an object has certain animal properties on the basis of how similar it is to people. For example, a 4-year-old might say that a dog breathes "because I do". A 5-year-old might explain that baby rabbits must inevitably grow "because, like me, if I were a rabbit, I would be five years old and become bigger and bigger".

The original data on early biological concepts came from a series of studies by Carey (1985). She asked 4-year-olds and 7-year-olds whether familiar and unfamiliar living things had biological properties, such as "eating", "having bones", "having babies" and "having a heart". The children were questioned about living things as diverse as hammerhead sharks, aardvarks, orchids and baobab trees, as well as more familiar species like dogs, fish, worms, flies and flowers. The experimental technique involved showing the children pictures of each living thing, and then asking them to make predictions about biological properties. Carey found that the attribution of every biological property fell off gradually across the animals as they became physically less similar to people, with the fly and the worm faring most poorly. Plants received very few attributions indeed. Within this gradient of physical similarity, there was no differentiation of biological properties. For example, the children were as willing to attribute "having bones" to flies and to worms as they were to attribute "having a heart". The older children (10-year-olds) did show differentiation between these properties. Carey argued that their biological knowledge was more adequate, as they had learned that while all animals share certain biological processes, they differ in their solutions to certain biological problems.

To test the idea that the children were using a people-based analogy to attribute biological properties to other animals, we need to study their patterns of projection for a completely unfamiliar biological property. If their projection of all biological properties is analogy-based, then the pattern of projection for an unfamiliar property should be the same as for a familiar one.

Carey tested this prediction by telling the children that every person has a spleen, and drawing a spleen in the appropriate place in a person's body. She then examined the children's ideas about which animals might be expected to have a spleen (dogs, aardvarks, worms, etc.). Once again, the patterns of attribution of the younger children were based on people as the prototypical owners of animal properties. In contrast, if taught that bees or dogs had spleens, the children were as likely to project spleens to inanimate objects such as vehicles and clouds as to animate objects like birds and people. The older children did not make these projection errors when taught about dogs and (to a lesser extent) bees. Having greater biological knowledge, they apparently saw people as one mammal among many, and so could use dogs as a basis for the projection of novel biological properties as well.

A different way of testing whether children base their biological inferences on analogies to people is to design an experiment in which *different* patterns of projection would be predicted on the basis of this analogy. This approach was taken by Inagaki and Hatano (1991), who asked 6-year-olds in Japan to predict the reactions of grasshoppers and potted tulips to three types of novel situation: being given too much to eat, being left behind in a shop and feeling sad when someone dies. They expected the three types of situation to lead to differential use of the people-based analogy. In the first type of situation, the analogy should be used, as predictions based on people would be correct. For example, if tulips get too much water, then they will die. In the second kind of situation, predictions based on people should contradict the children's knowledge about how the object actually behaves, and so a factual check should constrain the use of analogy. For example, a tulip would not protest at being left behind in a shop. In the third case, predictions based on people would simply be wrong. A grasshopper does not feel sad when someone dies, but children cannot observe this for themselves, and so a factual check will not constrain the use of analogy. In this situation, Inagaki and Hatano argued that the children should make incorrect analogies based on people, and say that tulips and grasshoppers have emotions (of course, many children's stories attribute emotional states to plants, animals and even inanimate objects, which could confuse the children).

As they expected, Inagaki and Hatano found that the children used the people analogy to a differential extent as long as they had the biological knowledge to check their analogy-based predictions. Although they made analogical projections to the tulip and to the grasshopper in the first and the third types of situation, saying that a tulip that was given too much water would "go bad", or that it would "feel sad inside" when someone died, they did not make such predictions in the second type of situation. Here, implausible predictions were rejected on the grounds of feasibility. For example, many children explained that the tulip and the grasshopper could not speak, and so could not protest at being left behind in a shop. Inagaki and Hatano concluded that because young children are so intimately familiar with humans while necessarily being ignorant of most other animate objects, they use their rich and flexible knowledge about humans as the source for analogical predictions and explanations about other animals.

So the early biological concept of animal seems to be based on an analogy to people, although in practice the analogy is constrained by factual knowledge about particular living things. With the development of increasing biological knowledge, the analogy is used less frequently. Carey has argued that this developmental change actually represents a conceptual shift in biological knowledge. She argues that the 10-year-old represents relations among biological processes that the 4-year-old does not, and so has a different conceptual system from that of the younger child. Between the ages of 4 and 10 years, biological knowledge becomes restructured so that the functions of eating, breathing and reproduction are understood in terms of maintaining life and the life cycle. Children thus infer that all animals must eat, breathe and reproduce, and they no longer attribute such properties on the basis of similarity to people. The 10-year-old should thus be able to make biological inferences and analogies that the younger child cannot.

## Analogies in Reading New Words

We turn now to a rather different area of classroom learning, namely learning to read. In fact, it was in trying to answer the question of how children might use analogies to help them to read new words that I first became interested in analogy.

When children use analogies to read unfamiliar written words, the important relations are those between spelling patterns and sound. The child makes an analogy between the spelling–sound relation of one word, for example "light", and the spelling–sound relation of another, unknown word, for example "fight". To derive the pronunciation of the unknown word by analogy to the known word, the child must recognise that the words share a spelling sequence (-ight), and must reason that therefore the words probably share a sound as well. The only extra knowledge needed to read the new word is then the sound of the first letter, which cannot be derived by analogy (here it would be /f/).

Work of my own has shown that beginning readers—children aged 5–6 years of age—are very good at making these kinds of analogies about spelling patterns (e.g. Goswami, 1986, 1987, 1988). In a typical experiment, children are taught a "clue" word as a basis for analogy, for example, "beak". They are then asked to read test words that are either analogous in spelling pattern to "beak" at the beginning (e.g. "bean", "bead", "beat") or at the end (e.g. "peak", "weak", "speak"). If they can use analogies to decode new words, then learning the "clue" word should enable them to infer the correct pronunciations of these test words, words that they were unable to read correctly prior to the experiment. To rule out the possibility that any improvement in reading the analogous words is due only to the number of letters shared between these words and the clue word, the children are also asked to read some non-analogous control words. There are usually more control words than analogous words, and some of the control words also share three letters with the clue word, although the shared letters are not in sequence (e.g. "bank", "bask"). A typical clue word experiment is depicted in Fig. 7.1.

In these experiments, the children consistently became able to read the analogous words after learning the clue words, but did not become able to read the non-analogous control words (e.g. Goswami, 1986, 1987, 1988). This difference was found whether the unknown words were presented to be read in isolation or were presented embedded in passages of prose. It was also found whether the words were printed in the same letter case as the clue words (a perceptual similarity manipulation) or were printed in a different letter case. The analogy effect did not depend on reading level or on age. The only factor that it did seem to depend on was shared spelling pattern. If the children were

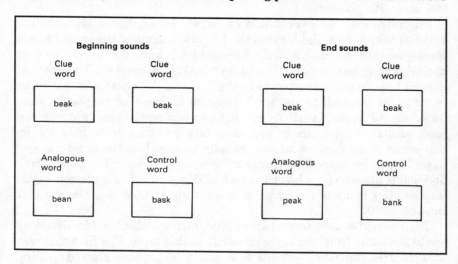

FIG. 7.1. Stimulus cards from a typical clue word experiment (Goswami, 1986) (Figure reproduced from Goswami & Bryant, 1990).

taught clue words for rhyming words that did not share the same spellings (e.g. "head"–"said"), then very little transfer was found.

A variety of experiments (see also Baron, 1977, 1979; Marsh, Friedman, Welch & Desberg, 1980) have thus established that children can use analogies in reading (*decoding* analogies). The relations in these analogies (those between the shared spelling patterns and the shared sounds of the words) seem to be fairly straightforward for most of the children to work out. However, some of the children found it quite difficult to use analogies to decode new words. To find out why this occurs, we must consider the relational knowledge on which decoding analogies seem to be based.

### Syllabic Structure and Analogies in Reading

In general terms, decoding analogies depend on systematic relationships between spelling patterns and sound. However, these spelling–sound relationships are not very systematic at the alphabetic level. Correspondences between alphabetic letters and single sounds, or *phonemes*, are very variable in written English. Although most consonant correspondences are systematic, most vowels are not (for example, consider the differing pronunciation of "o" in the words "one", "fox" and "gold"). Instead, a particular level of correspondence between letter *sequences* and sounds seems to be of most importance in decoding analogies. This *intra-syllabic* level relates parts of the syllable to sound, and allows far more consistency in spelling–sound relationships than is the case with phonemes.

The intra-syllabic level that is important for analogies concerns the division of spoken syllables into the linguistic units of the *onset* [a unit corresponding to the initial consonant(s)] and the *rime* [a unit corresponding to the vowel(s) and terminal consonant(s)]. The onset of a word like "beak" corresponds to the "b-" and the onset of a word like "spring" corresponds to the "spr-". The rime of "beak" corresponds to the "-eak" and of "spring" to the "-ing". In tasks testing the ability of children (and adults) to recognise or to manipulate sounds within the syllable, this *onset–rime division* has repeatedly emerged as the most natural basis for performance (see Treiman, 1988, for a review). The onset–rime division is also the only level at which children can divide spoken words into smaller units of sound prior to learning to read (see Goswami & Bryant, 1990).

Two clues about the importance of the intra-syllabic level for decoding analogies came from the early research on this topic. The first clue was that children consistently made more analogies between shared spelling patterns at the ends of words ("beak"–"peak") than between shared spelling patterns at the beginnings of words ("beak"–"bean"). So analogies based on rimes (e.g. "-eak") were easier than analogies based on the onset and part of the rime (e.g. "b-" + "-ea", giving the shared spelling sequence "bea-"). The second clue was that a child's rhyming skill was significantly related to that child's use of decoding analogies. Children who could categorise spoken words as "same" or "different" on the basis of rhyme were more likely to recognise that written words could be categorised as same or different on the basis of spelling pattern. These children were more likely to make analogies between written words than children who were not so good at categorising the sounds in spoken words (Goswami, 1990; Goswami & Mead, 1992).

The use of analogies in reading thus seems to depend on whether children's knowledge about spoken syllables includes awareness of the onset–rime division. If they are aware of this division, then they can make analogies from written to spoken language, and can use shared spelling patterns that reflect onset–rime units to read new words aloud (see also Goswami, 1991b). If their knowledge about syllable structure does not include knowledge of the onset–rime division, then they do not seem to use analogies between shared spelling sequences to decode new words in reading.

## Are Children Strategically Applying Analogies in Decoding?

The question of whether children are purposely using analogies between spelling patterns when they read is a difficult one to answer. I have tended to assume that they are not, for two reasons. First, in the single word experiments discussed earlier, most of the children did not use analogies consistently. Instead, they read some of the analogous test words correctly and made mistakes on others. This inconsistency in performance suggests that they were probably not consciously trying to apply an analogy strategy. However, some of the children *were* consistent in using analogies to read the test words, and they usually commented on their activity in some way. For example, they would tell the experimenter that the words were all the same. So some children do become aware that analogies can be applied strategically to read new words, and they will generally tell you so.

Secondly, when children were given stories to read that contained decoding analogies, they made almost as many analogies as they made in the single word experiments. In the latter, they were explicitly presented with the analogy, as a single clue and test word were presented in conjunction. In the story-reading experiments, the clue word was learned as part of the title of the story, and the test words were embedded in the story itself, so that the shared spelling patterns were never seen in conjunction with each other. However, this did not affect the level of analogising (Goswami, 1988). The robustness of the analogy effect across these two paradigms could be interpreted as evidence that children do not purposely make inferences about pronunciation when they use decoding analogies.

Children can be *taught* to use analogies purposely to help them in decoding, however, and this seems to help their reading progress. White and Cunningham (1990) have developed a programme for teaching children to read by analogy that can be used as part of normal classroom practice. Their study focused on minority and low-SES children aged 6–7 years, and the analogy decoding programme that they designed was administered by trained classroom teachers as part of the children's normal reading lessons.

The analogy programme was based on a "word wall", on which 200 words were arranged in alphabetical order, colour-coded by vowel. The words had largely been chosen to reflect major spelling patterns (e.g. "look"), so that they provided a base of words for analogy decoding. The children were first taught to read and to spell all of the words on this wall over a period of months. About a quarter of the way through the programme, which lasted for one year, they were introduced to the analogy strategy. The instruction about analogy began with some work on rhyming, and followed this up by systematically teaching the children about certain "word families", such as the "job", "nine" and "mat" families. To practise analogy, a new word like "spine" might be presented, and the children had to decide which column to write it in, and how it would be pronounced. This instruction about the categorisation and pronunciation of new words (which was also given in spelling) formed the majority of the analogy teaching programme.

A year later, the reading progress of the children in the classrooms that had used the analogy programme was compared to that of the children in the classrooms that had not. The children who had received training in analogy were found to have higher scores in standardised tests of both decoding and comprehension. White and Cunningham argued that their results showed that analogy decoding instruction was a very effective and practicable technique for teaching disadvantaged students. Gaskins, Downer and Gaskins (1986) have shown that a similar programme can also be very beneficial to dyslexic children. So although analogy seems to be a reading strategy that many children adopt spontaneously, it can also be taught to children, with useful results. I will return to the question of how conscious reflection on the usefulness of analogy might contribute to individual differences in using analogies later in this chapter.

Decoding is not the only skill that is important in becoming a good reader, however. An equally important skill is comprehension. Children need to be able to make sense of what they are reading as well as to be able to decode new written words. It turns out that analogy plays an important role in this aspect of reading as well.

## Analogies in Reading Comprehension

Analogies are potentially very useful for understanding new information presented in text. For example, if you are asked to comprehend the two sentences "The particles collided with each other" and "The particles collided with each other like billiard balls when the game has just begun" (Bean, Singer & Cowan, 1985), you will probably think that the second is easier to understand than the first. The image of billiard balls bouncing apart at random provides a vivid analogy for understanding how particles behave, and Bean et al. have claimed that the second sentence indeed makes the nature of particles much clearer to the novice reader of a physics text than the first.

Other research has confirmed that analogies do help students to comprehend difficult texts. For example, Hayes and Tierney (1982) found that baseball analogies were helpful to Californian students trying to understand passages about the game of cricket, and Simons (1984) developed a biscuit analogy to help students to understand the relationship between molecules, atoms and substance. The relationship between the whole biscuit, the crumbs and the ingredients was compared to the relationship between substance (the biscuit), molecules (the crumbs, which are the smallest part of the biscuit still having the same properties as the biscuit itself), and atoms (the ingredients of the biscuit).

Not all analogies in texts are beneficial, however. Spiro, Feltovich, Coulson and Anderson (1989) have pointed out the potentially misleading effects of many of the analogies used in medical textbooks. These are frequently only partial analogies, which often operate at the level of perceptual similarity rather than at the level of causal structure. Because of this, many medical students draw the wrong conclusions about body function from the analogies. For example, students are often told that the failing heart is analogous to a saggy balloon, which it resembles in appearance. Spiro et al. showed that such students mapped both similarity of appearance *and* similarity of causal mechanism from the balloon to the heart. They therefore wrongly assumed that tension in the heart wall decreased when the heart was failing, in the same way as tension in the balloon decreased when the balloon was losing air.

### Research with Children

Research into young children's ability to use analogies in reading comprehension is limited, however, perhaps because a certain stage of decoding must be reached before children can learn primarily from reading textbooks. However, younger children, too, should benefit from analogies when comprehending text, and at least two experiments have suggested that this is the case.

One experiment compared children's understanding of a human biology text either with or without the presence of a certain analogy. Vosniadou and Ortony (1983) looked at the effects of two different analogies on 6- and 8-year-old children's comprehension of human biology, a military analogy in a text about infection, and an economic analogy about the distribution of resources in a text about blood circulation. In the military analogy, the infection was compared to an enemy invading the body. The germs were analogous to the enemy forces, and the white blood cells were analogous to the army of defending soldiers. In the economic analogy, the human body was compared to a country containing people and factories that required food and fuel respectively. The blood circulation system was compared to the rail network in this country. The blood made "stops" at the stomach and kidneys in the same way as trains make stops at main-line stations, and carried food and fuel to individual body cells on the "branch lines" of smaller blood vessels.

To assess whether these analogies benefited the children's understanding of infection and blood circulation, control stories of equal length were designed which imparted the same factual information without the analogies. The children in the experiment either read the *Analogy* passages or the *No Analogy* passages, and then received some questions about infection and blood circulation to assess their comprehension. Some of these questions tested the children's understanding of the main ideas in the passages (factual), and others were inferential. The inferential questions assessed the understanding of causal consequences (e.g. "What can the body do to protect itself against infection?"), and also checked for possible analogical transfer errors such as those based on physical similarity (e.g. "Do the white cells use weapons to kill the germs?").

Vosniadou and Ortony found that the analogies did have a beneficial effect on the children's comprehension. The children in the Analogy Group remembered more about the passages than the children in the No Analogy Group, and they also knew significantly more of the answers to the factual questions. The 6-year-olds in the Analogy Group answered 31% and 49% of these questions correctly respectively (blood circulation and infection), compared to 22% and 27% for the No Analogy Group. Corresponding figures for the 8-year-olds were 41% and 59% correct for blood circulation and infection respectively, compared to 31% and 29% correct in the control group. The infection analogy was apparently more useful than the blood circulation analogy, as it led to greater gains in comprehension. So for younger children as well as for medical students, some analogies are better than others.

Another way of examining the role of analogy in reading comprehension is to see whether analogies *between* rather than within texts can benefit comprehension. Analogies may also emerge as part of a cumulative process of reading about different aspects of a particular topic. As more texts are studied, the knowledge base in a particular area should deepen, and various relationships that could support analogies should be acquired. These analogies would not be an explicit part of the texts themselves, but as the information necessary to draw analogies that will aid overall comprehension is gradually accumulated from reading related texts, we might expect the relevant analogies to be made spontaneously. Cumulative learning from texts is a very natural model of the classroom learning process.

*Collaborative Learning*

An experimental method for investigating cumulative learning has been developed by Brown and her colleague Palincsar. They have designed a method for teaching reading comprehension which they call *reciprocal teaching* (e.g. Palincsar & Brown, 1984). They have also been able to use this method to study children's use of analogies in reading comprehension. Originally designed to help backward readers, the reciprocal teaching method involves explicitly teaching groups of children to use particular strategies for understanding text, such as asking questions about the content of the text, and summarising the gist. The children are then helped to practise these strategies by taking it in turns to be the teacher of the reading group themselves. By presenting the reading groups with connected sets of texts that are based around a coherent theme, Brown and her colleagues can present the children with sets of examples of analogous problems and their solutions (e.g. Brown et al., 1991). Analogies between the texts are then found to emerge as a natural part of the cumulative learning process.

For example, in one set of stories based on classroom biology, the chosen themes were animal defence and survival mechanisms. The texts included topics such as camouflage and mimicry, natural pest control, parasites, protection from the elements, and extinction. On any one day, the children would read a passage about one of these topics, and would discuss and comprehend the passage using the reciprocal teaching strategies. They would then be given a test passage for comprehension that was directly analogous to the first passage. For example, a passage about manatees (the water mammals that eat weeds that clog inland waterways) might be followed by a test passage about the purple martin (the bird that eats mosquitoes; see also Chapter 5).

These topics would recur over 20 days of instruction, so that the children were receiving regular practice in comprehending information in text. During this time, Brown et al. recorded any examples of the children spontaneously using analogies to aid their comprehension. They found a graded analogy effect. For example, in a reading group of "at-risk" 8-year-olds, analogies were first made only between protagonists that appeared physically similar, such as ladybirds (which

TABLE 7.1

Dialogues from a Reading Group: Days 5 and 17[a]

**Day 5    Ladybugs**

| | |
|---|---|
| Student 1: | (Question) What do they eat? |
| Teacher: | What do what eat? |
| Student 1: | (Question) The ladybugs. What do ladybugs eat? |
| Student 2: | Aphids, little white bugs. |
| Student 1: | (Question) Right. Why do farmers like them? |
| Student 3: | Because they eat the little bugs off the farmers' plants. |
| Student 1: | That's the answer I want (pause). |
| Student 1: | (Question) I have another question. Where do they live? (overlapping discussion of potential places to live not accepted because they are not mentioned in the text) |
| Student 4: | I know, they crawl on leaves and rosebuds as in the grass. |
| Student 1: | (Summary) Okay. It's about the ladybugs that crawl in the grass and help the farmer by eating bad little insects. |
| Teacher: | Good summary. |

**Day 17    Manatees**

| | |
|---|---|
| Student 4: | (Question) How does the manatee clean up the river? |
| Student 3: | By eating water plants. |
| Student 4: | No, you missed one word. |
| Student 3: | By eating water hedge whatever. |
| Teacher: | Hyacinth. |
| Student 4: | Yea, that's right. |
| Student 4: | (Question) How many years ago people moved some of the manatees from the sea in the inland river. Amelia. |
| Student 6: | A few years. |
| Teacher: | (Scaffolding) Anne (S4) ... another way you could have asked that question would be ... when did the people move the manatees? |
| Student 4: | (Question) What did the people want the manatees to eat? |
| Student 2: | The plants. |
| Student 4: | I want the whole sentence. |
| Student 2: | The people wanted the manatees to eat the water hyacinths that grow in the river. |
| Student 4: | (Summary) Okay, that's it; it tells where the people moved them and what they wanted them to eat, and why. |
| Teacher: | Good summary. |
| Student 1: | (Noting analogy) The manatees went through and ate all the plants, so that's helping like the ladybugs because they eat all the aphids, bad bugs. |

[a] Brown et al. (1991). Reproduced with permission.

eat aphids) and the lacewing insect (which eats crop pests). As the children learned more about the material, they began to make analogies that did not depend on perceptual similarity, such as the analogy between the manatee and the purple house martin. After 10 days of instruction, the children were solving 90% of the analogous problems designed by Brown et al. by cross-reference to the discussion passages. The children were also spontaneously making analogies between stories presented in different sessions (e.g. days 5 and 17; see Table 7.1).

Strikingly, a follow-up study conducted a year later showed that the children were able to remember analogies that were presented a year apart. They were also able to sort pictures of the animals into sets representing the different biological themes (i.e. into sets for mimicry, camouflage, extinction, etc.), to provide a justification for why a particular animal represented that theme, and to discuss the analogous relation, even though they had learned this information a whole year previously. They could even classify novel exemplars of the themes, and place them in the appropriate habitats. Their retention of so much information over a whole year is strong evidence that the comprehension gains that resulted from the use of analogy were genuine. So children use analogies in reading as a natural mechanism for acquiring and organising knowledge in *both* decoding and comprehension.

## A FAILURE OF SPONTANEOUS ANALOGY: ANALOGIES IN LEARNING MATHEMATICS

Do children show the same facility in using analogies when they are learning mathematics? This is an important question, as analogy is widely used in mathematics teaching. The analogy usually takes the form of a concrete representation of the concept to be taught. For example, in the primary or kindergarten classroom, children are given Dienes blocks or Unifix cubes (plastic cubes that fit together in multiples of ten) to represent the decimal number system, and are encouraged to use these to work out simple addition and subtraction problems. The assumption is that the blocks will help the children to understand decimal notation. Older children may be given analogies based on pies or cakes to learn about fractions. The pies and cakes are meant to help the children to understand that fractions are sub-parts of the whole.

The most interesting point about these analogies is the teacher's assumption that children will spontaneously be able to make the link between the concrete representation and the target concept. This is a rather different assumption from that found in most of the research on analogical reasoning. To the teacher, the analogy is transparent, and merely provides a tool for conceptual understanding. But how transparent is the analogy to the child?

The answer seems to be, not very. At least two sets of research into mathematical development have suggested that the commonly-used concrete analogies selected here are not at all transparent to the children that they are intended to help.

## Understanding Decimal Notation and the Number Operations

The widespread use of Dienes blocks in the primary classroom is a good example of an analogy that is not as transparent as it seems. Dienes blocks are meant to provide a concrete analogue of the written symbols representing the numbers, and of the operations on numbers (addition, subtraction, multiplication and division). However, children seem to have a great deal of difficulty in understanding that the blocks provide them with analogies to the sums that they have been given to solve.

For example, Hughes (1986) asked children aged 5–7 years to use small bricks to represent different sums written on cards. The sums were represented numerically, and were very simple: "3 + 4 = 7" and "6 – 2 = 4". A single card with "5" written on it was also used. The children were told "I want you to show me what's on the card, show me what it means, using bricks" (p. 98).

To Hughes' surprise, the children did not find this task trivially easy. Only 27% of them used the bricks to represent the sums (for example, by adding a group of 3 bricks to a group of 4 bricks to make 7 bricks). Many children represented the operators (+, =) literally, for example by using bricks to build up the shape of a plus sign, and one child even used 11 bricks to form the shape of the numeral "5".

Can we be sure that the children understood Hughes' task? In a more "child-friendly" version of this study, Stallard (1982) asked 60 children aged 6–10 years to explain simple sums written on cards to a toy panda. The panda was introduced as needing their help because he did not understand things very easily. Stallard used a larger variety of sums than Hughes, although the largest numeral in these sums was also "6" (5 + 6 = 11).

She found that some sums were easier to represent with bricks than others. Approximately 60% of the children could manage the sums "5 – 5 = 0", "2 + 2 = 4", "3 – 1 = 2" and "1 + 3 = 4", and about 45% could represent sums written in a less conventional fashion ("4 = 6 – 2" and "7 = 5 + 2"). Only a third of the children could represent "4 + 0 = 4", however, and only 18% could represent "3 = 3". The children who were rated by their teachers as "good" at mathematics performed significantly better at all ages than those rated as "average" or "poor". Of course, the "good" children may have already had extensive practice in using blocks. So all that we can conclude from this study is that the children who understood the concepts represented by the sums could construct the analogies.

Do these experiments necessarily imply that bricks or blocks are not useful analogues for the number operations? Although Hughes was not actually looking at analogy in his studies, he does not think so. He comments: "In order to solve practical mathematical problems, we need to be capable … of making fluent translations between formal and concrete representations of the same problem. … While we as adults can see the advantages of being on the other side [of the bridge between formal and concrete representations], the children themselves may not" (pp. 169–170). However, we know from previous research that translation itself is not a problem if the children understand the relations on which an analogy is based.

We are left with two possibilities. One is that there may be better concrete analogies than blocks or bricks for teaching children about the number operations. Blocks and bricks may just seem like obvious materials to use to represent numbers to adults. The other is that although the manipulation of blocks or bricks is actually quite a good way of teaching children about the number operations, the understanding that the numbers *represent* the bricks (or any other real entity that can be counted) may only emerge slowly and with extensive practice, at least for the majority of children. If children do not understand the relationship between the numbers and the bricks, then they will not be able to use the bricks to learn about the number operations.

We already know from Deloache's work (Chapter 6) that young children have difficulty in understanding what it is to represent. If younger children do lack "representational insight", then this might impede their use of concrete analogies like bricks and blocks. To translate from concrete to abstract representations of number, the children must first understand that the numbers represent the Dienes blocks. If the barrier to learning is indeed one of representational insight, then the first step in using such concrete analogues should be to teach children about the representational relationship.

*Embedded Knowledge and Concrete Analogies*
The use of these concrete analogies may also impede the development of mathematical understanding in quite another way. Many children may initially develop two different and quite separate systems of knowledge about the number system, one based on concrete materials,

and one based on written problems. The understanding of the number system that develops through the use of Dienes blocks might be deeply *embedded* in the context of the concrete manipulations and, as far as the child is concerned, inseparable from it. Transfer of knowledge about the number system from blocks to written sums would then be very difficult.

A detailed investigation of children's errors in subtraction has suggested that such contextual embedding may be quite frequent, and may indeed be difficult to overcome (Resnick & Omanson, 1987). In a fascinating and comprehensive study, Resnick and Omanson investigated 8-year-old children's knowledge of the subtraction principles, using both concrete materials and written sums. The concrete materials were Dienes blocks, bundles of wooden rods (1 bundle = 10 rods) and coloured chips. Subtraction knowledge was tested by a variety of different tasks, including asking the children to "read" displays of possible concrete representations (e.g. 8 bundles of 10 rods and 3 single rods would be read as "83"), asking the children to construct displays of different numbers (e.g. "use blocks to show the number 256") and asking them to show a quantity in two ways (e.g. "12" could be shown as a ten block and two unit blocks, or as 12 single units). The written tasks included comparing the value of the same digit appearing in two different columns (e.g. 3 in 23 and 3 in 322), subtracting with borrowing using paper and pencil, and naming the place value of borrowing marks (e.g. borrowing a "1" from the tens column in the sum 322–129).

Resnick and Omanson found that the children performed well in the concrete tasks, but were markedly weaker in the written tasks. For example, even though all of the children could represent the decimal system with the concrete materials, only one child could reliably compare the value of the same digit when it appeared in different columns in the written problems. Even at the end of the school year, these children were having difficulty in interpreting the value of the numbers that were being borrowed from different columns.

Resnick and Omanson concluded that the children had a far better command of the decimal value system when they were using block representations than when they were operating on written representations. The children seemed to have a good understanding of the mathematical principles underlying subtraction in one case, but not in the other. In fact, Resnick and Omanson noted that the children did not seem to see any connection between what they were learning with the blocks and what they were learning about the written sums, even though they had become very adept at solving problems with the concrete materials. This inability to see a connection between the blocks and the written sums was attributed to "very weak mapping between the individual elements of the two representational systems ... children's capabilities for doing arithmetic with blocks was not reflected in a comparable ability for doing written arithmetic problems" (p. 64).

To try and overcome this weakness in the understanding of the relational correspondences between the two systems, Resnick and Omanson decided to try to explicitly teach the children to map their knowledge from one representation to the other, hoping thereby to facilitate analogical transfer. To this end, they developed a technique called "mapping instruction". During mapping instruction, the experimenter ensured that a step-by-step correspondence was maintained between the blocks and the written symbols throughout the solution of each problem. An example of this is shown in Fig. 7.2. The explicit focus on the 1:1 correspondence between the blocks and the written sums was expected to help the children to transfer their knowledge about the subtraction principles from the concrete materials to the written arithmetic.

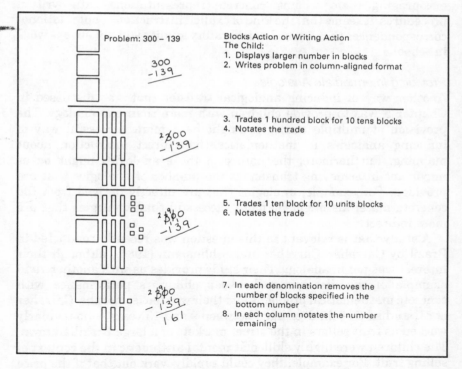

FIG. 7.2. An example of mapping instruction (reproduced with permission from Resnick & Omanson, 1987).

Surprisingly, however, the mapping instruction was largely unsuccessful. Children who showed a high level of understanding of the principles underlying subtraction when they were using the blocks continued to make many errors in their written calculations. The reason was apparently that they already had relatively automatic (although flawed) calculation routines for written arithmetic. They continued to use these routines to perform the written calculations despite the experimenters' attempts to make them reflect on their concrete knowledge about mathematical principles. This is a classic example of *negative learning set*. The children had developed one set of routines to use with written sums and another set to use with blocks, and their prior learning with written arithmetic impeded analogical transfer from the blocks.

The conclusion from Resnick and Omanson's work would seem to be that it is very difficult to disembed knowledge that has been overlearned in the classroom via direct instruction. Although it remains possible that there may be better analogies than blocks or bricks for teaching children about the number operations (fingers, perhaps?), and better ways of encouraging them to link concrete representations with written procedures, it seems that the kind of explicit instruction about relational correspondences that worked in laboratory studies will not always work in school.

*Providing Intermediate Analogies*

Another way of inducing analogical transfer that was discussed in Chapter 5 was to provide children with more than one analogy. The provision of multiple analogies might be a more successful way of inducing analogies in mathematics than direct instruction about mapping. Furthermore, the nature of these analogies might be as important in achieving transfer as the number of analogies that are provided. For example, analogies that are directly derived from the concrete materials might be more successful than analogies that are more indirect.

A study that is relevant to this question was recently conducted in Brazil by Carraher, Carraher and Schliemann (1985), although their interest was not in analogy. Their study provides us with another vivid example of the discrepancy between children's performance with concrete mathematical problems and their written isomorphs. Carraher et al. studied five children aged between 9 and 15 years, who regularly worked as fruit sellers in the street markets of a large Brazilian town. The children were highly skilled at mental arithmetic in the context of selling fruit. For example, they could rapidly work out that if the price of one coconut was 35 cruzeiro (the Brazilian currency), then 10 coconuts would cost 350 cruzeiro. A complex combination of multiplication and addition was typically used in calculating these sums: For example, a 12-year-old solved the coconut problem by working out that three coconuts would cost 105 cruzeiro, so six would be 210 cruzeiro, nine would be 315 cruzeiro, and one more would make 350 cruzeiro.

In order to test each child's mental arithmetic informally, the researchers first posed as customers buying fruit. As customers, they set the young vendors various mental arithmetic problems of the kind described above. They then revealed themselves to be researchers, and asked the children to complete a written paper and pencil test made up of exactly the same calculations. This test was developed independently for each child. For example, the written sums for the child who made the calculation mentioned above might include 35 x 10, 35 x 3, 105 + 105, and 315 + 35.

Carraher et al. found that the children's performance in the written tests was extremely poor, even though the tests required exactly the same mathematical calculations as the transactions with fruit. Performance on the paper and pencil tests averaged 41% correct, compared to an average of 98% correct when using mental arithmetic in the street market. The children seemed to treat their fruit-selling activities as entirely separate from classroom mathematics, and were apparently oblivious to the relationship between the two. They did not recognise the correspondence between the two sets of problems.

Furthermore, as in Resnick and Omanson's study, the children seemed to have one set of procedures for the marketplace and a different set for the classroom. In the formal paper and pencil test, they attempted to use what Carraher et al. called "school-taught routines", and made many mistakes. In the marketplace, they used a flexible and creative system of mental arithmetic that they had developed for themselves. The challenge for the researchers was to make them realise that this system was relevant to their classroom mathematics.

To try and help the children to apply their market knowledge to the written sums, Carraher et al. decided to present the same written problems in a story format (e.g. Mary had x bananas, each banana cost y, how much did she pay altogether?). This provided a direct analogy to the marketplace. With this new version of the written test, average performance leaped to 75% correct. While it remains puzzling that performance with this direct analogy was not even higher, the improvement found in the children's written arithmetic is encouraging. It suggests that it may be possible to encourage children to disembed knowledge gained from concrete experience if some kind of intermediate analogy is used to facilitate transfer. An important next step in testing this hypothesis would be to examine transfer from the written problems to the written sums, which Carraher et al. did not do.

*Understanding Fractions*

Fractions is another area of mathematics in which concrete analogies are widely used in teaching. Perhaps the most frequently-used analogy here is the "sub-area of a whole" analogy. In this analogy, fractions like ½ or ¼ are compared to portions of whole cakes or whole pies. A different analogy is the "subset–set comparison". In this analogy, a subset of discrete objects is compared to the whole set. For example, if 2 eggs in a carton of 6 are brown, then ⅓ of the eggs are brown.

Research has shown that even adolescents have difficulty in understanding how fractions can be used to represent these concrete analogies. For example, a British survey of primary school pupils (Department of Education & Science, 1980) found that only 64% of 11-year-olds could solve a problem in which they were given 3 yellow tiles and 1 red tile, and were asked what fraction of the squares were red, a very simple version of the subset–set analogy. In a separate study, Hart (1980) investigated 12-year-old-children's understanding of the following question: "5 eggs in a box of 12 are found to be cracked. What fraction of the box of eggs is cracked?" She found that 30% of the children were unable to solve this problem correctly. She also found that 39% of this age group could not shade in ⅔ of a hexagon that was marked off in sixths (the "sub-area of a whole" analogy).

If older children have difficulty in understanding concrete analogies for very simple fractions, then how do younger children fare? The answer seems to be, not very well. Gelman, Cohen and Hartnett (1989, cited in Gelman, 1991) asked children aged 5–7 years to place concrete representations of fractions in the correct position on a "number line". This 4 ft 4 inch line was laid out on the floor, with the integers 1–3 marked by one circle, two circles and three circles. The fractions were represented concretely by segments of circles printed on cards, such as a half-segment of a circle, a segment of a third of a circle, a whole circle and a segment of a third of a circle (representing the fraction 1⅓, which would be two pieces), and so on. The children were given these different pieces to position in the appropriate spatial locations on the number line, so that the half circle would be put between 0 and 1, the whole-circle-and-a-third between 1 and 2, and so on. The number line task is shown in Fig. 7.3.

The children that Gelman et al. tested were very poor at this task. Only 23% of them managed to produce the correct responses. The most common error was to order the segments by counting (e.g. ⅓ was placed at 1 because it was a single shape, 1⅓ was placed at 2 because it was 2 shapes, and so on). Gelman (1991) concluded that young children viewed number as something that you can count, and so tried to integrate the concrete analogies of the fractions with the count laws. This led them

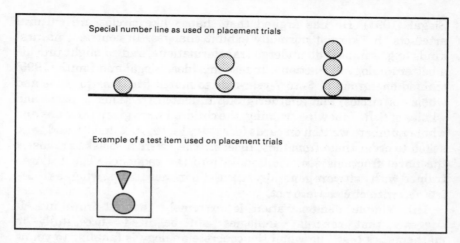

Special number line as used on placement trials

Example of a test item used on placement trials

FIG. 7.3. The Number Line Task (reproduced with permission from Gelman, 1991).

to make errors on the number line, and to draw erroneous conclusions about written fractions, such as that ¼ was bigger than ½ (as 4 is bigger than 2).

This "counting" explanation might also provide an insight into the difficulties that children have in using portions of pie or cake as analogies of fractions. Young children probably have a lot of experience of the division of pies or of cakes at home, but they may not think of the resulting pieces as sub-parts of the whole pie or cake. Instead, they may focus on the *number* of pieces created by the division (e.g. 4 pieces of pie instead of 4 quarters). Although they are aware that the pie is being shared out, they might think of sharing in terms of the number of recipients. Clearly, unless they think about sharing in terms of equal subdivisions of the whole, then they will not be thinking about fractions but about something that you can count.

If this idea is correct, then the use of pies and cakes as concrete analogies of fractions may actually *mislead* children. The pie analogy might cause them to focus on the number of pieces of pie rather than on the division of the whole pie or cake, resulting in negative analogical transfer to the fractions. This idea would be simple to test. If children do not think about sub-parts of the whole when they see cakes and pies being divided, then they should judge unfair divisions of pies and cakes (e.g. into four unequal pieces) as acceptable quarters, and they should not distinguish them from fair divisions into equal quarters.

A different explanation for why segments of circles are not good "sub-area of the whole" analogies to fractions has been proposed by

Siegal (1991). He has argued that shapes like circles are cultural artefacts that do not normally exhibit changes. In contrast, natural kinds (e.g. animals) do undergo transformations, and so might provide a better analogy to fractions. To test this idea, Siegal and Smith (1990) trained one group of 6- to 7-year-olds to match fractions to parts and wholes of circles, and another group to match fractions to parts and wholes of fish. Following training, the children were given fractions and whole numbers written on cards (0, 1/7, 1/6, 1/4, 1/2, 1, 2 and 3), and were asked to order them from most to least. They were also asked to insert the novel fractions 1/20, 1/10 and 1/8 into the sequence. The children trained with fish were generally successful in these tasks, whereas those trained with circles were not.

This simple demonstration is extremely thought-provoking. It suggests that concrete analogies can be used successfully in mathematics teaching when the concrete analogy is familiar to young children. If the children do not have to learn about the analogy as well as about the concept that it is intended to represent, then representational insight (and analogical transfer) may be automatic. With other concrete analogies, such as segments of circles, children may need help in understanding the representing function of the analogy. Fish may provide better analogies to fractions than segments of circles because children already understand that pictures of animals represent the real thing. Understanding that fractions represent the parts of the fish may then be a comparatively small step to take (even though a fish dividing into half is not a natural transformation!).

An interesting extension of Siegal and Smith's work would be to use toy animals (say, small toy cats) instead of Dienes blocks to teach young children about the number operations. It may turn out that with natural kinds as analogies, children would be able to represent the kinds of arithmetical problems studied by Hughes and by Stallard, problems that they could not represent with blocks. If Siegal's idea about natural kinds is correct, then there should be a significant advantage of animals over blocks. However, it may also have been important for the success of Siegal and Smith's fish analogy that the children in their study did not seem to possess overlearned classroom procedures for solving problems with fractions.

The message seems to be that to teach mathematics with concrete analogies, it is important to use familiar analogies, and to begin early. Children must be taught procedures with concrete materials before (or as) they learn about written representations, so that they do not develop parallel systems of embedded knowledge. The analogies must also be based on familiar materials, so that the analogy is transparent. When analogies are unfamiliar, then children seem to have difficulty in understanding the representing function of the concrete materials, and this impedes transfer to the intended mathematical concepts.

## Summary

The laboratory studies of reasoning by analogy have turned out to have a direct application to the classroom. The themes that emerged from the laboratory research—the importance of relational knowledge, the insight that not all knowledge was equal, and the necessity of disembedding relational knowledge from its context if analogies were to be used—have all played an important role in the use of analogies in classroom learning. The different methods for inducing analogy that were discovered in the laboratory—the use of hints, the use of direct instructions, the provision of more than one analogy—and the possible drawbacks of misleading analogies, also turned out to be directly applicable to classroom teaching.

The role of relational knowledge in successful classroom analogies probably provides the most direct link between theory and practice. In this book, I have argued that children should be able to use analogies whenever they understand the relations on which an analogy is based, as long as performance factors do not intervene. In classroom learning, this means that as long as the children have sufficient knowledge about the basis for the analogy (for example, about people for the biological analogies, or about fish for the mathematical analogies), then they should make correct predictions about the target (the possession of a spleen in biology, or the spatial location of fractions on a number line in mathematics). This seems to be the case.

A reasonably direct link between theory and practice is also found if the role of different *kinds* of knowledge in classroom analogies is considered. We saw in Chapter 5 that analogies are used spontaneously in learning if they are based on a coherent system of knowledge, and this certainly seemed to determine the use of analogies in reading. In decoding, knowledge about the relational structure of the spoken syllable (specifically about onsets and rimes) provided a basis for predictions about the pronunciations of the spelling patterns representing these units in unknown words. In reading comprehension, the gradual accumulation of knowledge about a causally rich domain (biology) resulted in the spontaneous use of analogies to make sense of new information about this domain, or to solve new problems set within it. So the possession of coherent knowledge systems did seem to govern the use of analogies in reading and in biology.

In mathematics, however, the analogies that were used seemed to be based on knowledge that was, for the children, partial or fragmentary, and in these circumstances transfer was very difficult to induce. The children in the studies that we reviewed did not really seem to understand how segments of circles represented sub-parts of a whole circle, or how operations with Dienes blocks were related to operations with written numbers. Therefore, they did not use analogies based on the blocks or on the segments of circles to help them to understand the mathematical concepts that they were being taught.

In some cases, their difficulties were due to the embedding of knowledge in a specific context. Although the children had a lot of knowledge about the base in some of the analogies, for example about manipulating Dienes blocks or about calculating fruit prices in the Brazilian market study, this knowledge tended to remain firmly embedded in the concrete situation in which it was learned. To make things worse, the children were often simultaneously developing a completely separate set of procedures to use in the target domain (written arithmetic), which also impeded transfer from the concrete analogies. The children were developing one set of procedures for the concrete materials and a completely different set of procedures for the written problems, and the two procedures were remaining independent. Clearly, it is much harder for children to use analogies if they also have a highly-practised set of erroneous routines that the analogy needs to supplant.

In other cases, their acquisition of the mathematical concepts was impeded because the children's partial understanding of the required knowledge base resulted in negative transfer. For example, they seemed to know that segments of a circle were something that you could count, and this knowledge prevented them from understanding the "sub-part of a whole" analogy between the segments and the fractional notation that they were being taught. As their knowledge about the basis for the analogy was not coherent in these different areas of mathematics, the spontaneous analogical transfer found in reading and in biology was unfortunately absent.

Similar difficulties can be shown to arise with analogies in reading and in biology, however, and so they may not be insurmountable in mathematics. For example, many studies of reading development have shown that knowledge about phonology is deeply embedded in knowledge about spoken language. In order to learn to read efficiently, children (and illiterate adults) need to disembed this knowledge, and to become "phonologically aware". For example, they must become aware that there are units of sound that are smaller than the syllable, such as onsets, rimes and phonemes. In order to gain phonological awareness, children can be helped to reflect on their knowledge about phonology, and various techniques have been devised to teach them to do so (see

Goswami & Bryant, 1990). So the problem of disembedding the appropriate knowledge in order to benefit from analogies is not unique to mathematics. Children may need to extract the relevant relations from the context in which they have been learned to make analogies in reading as well, or to conceptualise knowledge that they already have in a new way.

This problem about restructuring knowledge before analogy can be used highlights a very interesting question for research, one that I believe is the next important issue in our understanding of the development of analogical reasoning, and one that is particularly related to the question of how analogies might cause intellectual development. This is the question of whether analogies can ever enable genuinely *new* learning. In the research that has been considered in this book, the use of analogy has usually depended on seeing correspondences between conceptual relationships that have already been represented in the knowledge base. If these relationships have not already been represented, then the child has received explicit help in restructuring his or her knowledge in such a way that the important relations emerge. This raises the question of what would happen if one had no conceptual understanding of a domain at all. In these circumstances, it seems unlikely that analogies from a familiar domain could help in learning about the new domain. Current research suggests that analogies will only aid new learning once at least some of the fundamental relationships in the new domain have been acquired.

The role of analogy in the history of science supports the idea that analogies are only used once a certain degree of knowledge about a domain has already been acquired. We saw at the beginning of this book that Kepler was in some sense mentally "set up" to make his analogy about celestial mechanics, as he already knew most of the relationships in the puzzle. His analogy between God and the Sun enabled him to *restructure* knowledge that he already possessed about the planets and their motion into a new and superior conceptual system, with the resulting emergence of new superordinate concepts such as gravity. So Kepler's analogy enabled conceptual change, resulting in the representation of different relations among familiar concepts. This new pattern of relationships led to the emergence of a new causal explanatory system. Such restructuring of knowledge is clearly extremely powerful, and can lead to genuinely new insights and discoveries. The challenge for research is to discover how analogies can be used in the classroom. We need to help children to make the same conceptual leaps and discoveries that scientists have made before them as we teach them the knowledge that their culture has acquired about the world.

# References

Achenbach, T.M. (1970). Standardisation of a research instrument for identifying associative responding in children. *Developmental Psychology, 2,* 283–291.

Achenbach, T.M. (1971). The children's associative responding test: A two-year follow-up. *Journal of Educational Psychology, 61,* 340–348.

Alexander, P.A., Willson, V.L., White, C.S., & Fuqua, J.D. (1987a). Analogical reasoning in young children. *Journal of Educational Psychology, 79,* 401–408.

Alexander, P.A., Wilson, A.F., White, C.S., Willson, V.L., Tallent, M.K., & Shutes, R.E. (1987b). Effects of teacher training on children's analogical reasoning performance. *Teaching and Teacher Education, 3,* 275–285.

Alexander, P.A., White, C.S., Haensly, P., & Crimmins-Jeanes, M. (1987c). Training in analogical reasoning. *American Education Research Journal, 24,* 387–404.

Alexander, P.A., Willson, V.L., White, C.S., Fuqua, J.D., Clark, G.D., Wilson, A.F., & Kulikowich, J.M. (1989). Development of analogical reasoning in 4- and 5-year-old children. *Cognitive Development, 4,* 65–88.

Baillargeon, R. (1987). Object permanence in 3.5- and 4.5-month-old infants. *Developmental Psychology, 23,* 655–664.

Baillargeon, R. (1991). *Infants' reasoning about collision events.* Paper presented at the Biennial Meeting of the Society for Research in Child Development, Seattle, WA., April.

Baillargeon, R. (in press). The development of infants' physical reasoning. In H.W. Reese (Ed.), *Advances in child development and behaviour,* Vol. 23. New York: Academic Press.

Baillargeon, R. & DeVos, J. (1991). Object permanence in young infants: Further evidence. *Child Development, 62,* 1227–1246.

Baillargeon, R., Spelke, E.S., & Wasserman, S. (1985). Object permanence in 5-month-olds. *Cognition, 20,* 191–208.

Baron, J. (1977). Mechanisms for pronouncing printed words: Use and acquisition. In D. LaBerge & S.J. Samuels (Eds.), *Basic processes in reading: Perception and comprehension*, pp. 175–216. Hillsdale, N.J.: Lawrence Erlbaum Associates Inc.

Baron, J. (1979). Orthographic and word specific mechanisms in children's reading of words. *Child Development, 50*, 60–72.

Bauer, P.J. & Mandler, J.M. (1989). Taxonomies and triads: Conceptual organisation in one- to two-year olds. *Cognitive Psychology, 21*, 156–184.

Bean, T.W., Singer, H., & Cowan, S. (1985). Analogical study guides: Improving comprehension in science. *Journal of Reading*, December, 246–250.

Bisanz, J., Bisanz, G., & LeFevre, F. (1984). Interpretation of instructions: A source of individual differences in analogical reasoning. *Intelligence, 8*, 161–177.

Brown, A.L. (1982). Learning and development: The problem of compatibility, access and induction. *Human Development, 25*, 89–115.

Brown, A.L. (1986). *Learning and transfer in children: Domain-specific principles and domain-general strategies*. Paper presented at the Psychonomic Society, New Orleans, November 1986.

Brown, A.L. (1989). Analogical learning and transfer: What develops? In S. Vosniadou & A. Ortony (Eds.), *Similarity and analogical reasoning*, pp. 369–412. Cambridge: Cambridge University Press.

Brown, A.L. (1990). Domain-specific principles affect learning and transfer in children. *Cognitive Science, 14*, 107–133.

Brown, A.L., Campione, J.C., Reeve, R.A., Ferrara, R.A., & Palincsar, A.S. (1991). Interactive learning, individual understanding: The case of reading and mathematics. In L.T. Landsmann (Ed.), *Culture, schooling and psychological development*, pp. 136-170. Norwood, N.J.: Ablex Publishing Corp.

Brown, A.L. & Kane, M.J. (1988). Preschool children can learn to transfer: Learning to learn and learning by example. *Cognitive Psychology, 20*, 493–523.

Brown, A.L., Kane, M.J., & Echols, C.H. (1986). Young children's mental models determine analogical transfer across problems with a common goal structure. *Cognitive Development, 1*, 103–121.

Brown, A.L., Kane, M.J., & Long, C. (1989). Analogical transfer in young children: Analogies as tools for communication and exposition. *Applied Cognitive Psychology, 3*, 275–293.

Bryant, P.E. (1974). *Perception and understanding in young children*. London: Methuen.

Bullock, M., Gelman, R., & Baillargeon, R. (1982). Development of causal reasoning. In J.W. Friedman (Ed.), *Psychology of time*, pp. 209–254. New York: Academic Press.

Carey, S. (1985). *Conceptual change in childhood*. Cambridge, Mass.: MIT Press.

Carraher, T.N., Carraher, D.W., & Schliemann, A.D. (1985). Mathematics in the streets and in schools. *British Journal of Developmental Psychology, 3*, 21–30.

Chen, Z. & Daehler, M.W. (1989). Positive and negative transfer in analogical problem-solving. *Cognitive Development, 4*, 327–344.

Cooper, R.G. (1984). Early number development: Discovering number space with addition and subtraction. In C. Sophian (Ed.), *The origins of cognitive skills*, pp. 157–192. Hillsdale, N.J.: Lawrence Erlbaum Associates Inc.

Das Gupta, P. & Bryant, P.E. (1989). Young children's causal inferences. *Child Development, 60*, 1138–1146.

Deloache, J.S. (1987). Rapid change in the symbolic functioning of very young children. *Science, 238,* 1556–1557.

Deloache, J.S. (1989). Young children's understanding of the correspondence between a scale model and a larger space. *Cognitive Development, 4,* 121–139.

Deloache, J.S. (1990). Young children's understanding of models. In R. Fivush & J. Hudson (Eds.), *Knowing and remembering in young children* (pp.94–126). New York: Cambridge University Press.

Department of Education and Science (1980). *Mathematical development, Primary Survey Report No. 1.* London: HMSO.

Gallagher, J.M. & Wright, R.J. (1977). *Children's solution of verbal analogies: Extension of Piaget's concept of reflexive abstraction.* Paper presented to the Society for Research in Child Development, New Orleans.

Gallagher, J.M. & Wright, R.J. (1979). Piaget and the study of analogy: Structural analysis of items. In J. Magary (Ed.), *Piaget and the helping professions,* Vol. 8, pp. 114–119. Los Angeles: University of Southern California.

Gaskins, I.W., Downer, M.A., & Gaskins, R.W. (1986). *Introduction to the Benchmark School word identification/vocabulary development program.* Media, PA: Benchmark Press.

Gelman, R. (1991). Epigenetic foundations of knowledge structures: Initial and transcendent constructions. In S. Carey & R. Gelman (Eds.), *The epigenesis of mind: Essays on biology and cognition,* pp. 293–322. Hillsdale, N.J.: Lawrence Erlbaum Associates Inc.

Gelman, R., Cohen, M., & Hartnett, P. (1989). *To know mathematics is to go beyond thinking that "fractions aren't numbers".* Proceedings of the Eleventh Annual Meeting of the North American Chapter, International Group for Psychology of Mathematics Education. New Brunswick, N.J.

Gentile, J.R., Kessler, D.K., & Gentile, P.K. (1969). Process of solving analogy items. *Journal of Educational Psychology, 60,* 494–502.

Gentile, J.R., Tedesco-Stratton, L., Davis, E., Lund, N.J., & Agunanne, B.A. (1977). Associative responding versus analogical reasoning by children. *Intelligence, 1,* 369–380.

Gentner, D. (1983). Structure-mapping: A theoretical framework for analogy. *Cognitive Science, 7,* 155–170.

Gentner, D. (1988). Metaphor as structure-mapping: The relational shift. *Child Development, 59,* 47–59.

Gentner, D. (1989). The mechanisms of analogical learning. In S. Vosniadou & A. Ortony (Eds.), *Similarity and analogical reasoning,* pp. 199–241. Cambridge: Cambridge University Press.

Gentner, D. & Ratterman, M.J. (1992). Language and the career of similarity. In S.A. Gelman & J.P. Byrnes (Eds.), *Perspectives on thought and language: Inter-relations in development,* pp. 225-277. Cambridge: Cambridge University Press.

Gentner, D. & Toupin, C. (1986). Systematicity and surface similarity in the development of analogy. *Cognitive Science, 10,* 277–300.

Gentner, D., Ratterman, M.J., & Campbell, R. (in prep.). *Evidence for a relational shift in the development of analogical processing: A reply to Goswami & Brown.* Department of Psychology, Northwestern University, Ill.

Gholson, B., Eymard, L.A., Morgan, D., & Kamhi, A.G. (1987). Problem solving, recall and isomorphic transfer among third-grade and sixth-grade children. *Journal of Experimental Child Psychology, 43,* 227–243.

Gick, M.L. & Holyoak, K.J. (1980). Analogical problem solving. *Cognitive Psychology, 12*, 306–355.

Gick, M.L. & Holyoak, K.J. (1983). Schema induction and analogical transfer. *Cognitive Psychology, 15*, 1–38.

Goldman, S.R. & Pellegrino, J.W. (1984). Deductions about induction: Analyses of developmental and individual differences. In R.J. Sternberg (Ed.), *Advances in the psychology of human intelligence*, Vol. 2, pp. 149–197. Hillsdale, N.J.: Lawrence Erlbaum Associates Inc.

Goldman, S.R., Pellegrino, J.W., Parseghian, P.E., & Sallis, R. (1982). Developmental and individual differences in verbal analogical reasoning. *Child Development, 53*, 550–559.

Gordon, W.J.J. (1979). Some source material in discovery-by-analogy. *Journal of Creative Behaviour, 8*, 239–257.

Goswami, U. (1986). Children's use of analogy in learning to read: A developmental study. *Journal of Experimental Child Psychology, 42*, 73–83.

Goswami, U. (1987). *Children's use of analogy in reading and spelling.* Unpublished D. Phil. thesis, University of Oxford.

Goswami, U. (1988). Orthographic analogies and reading development. *Quarterly Journal of Experimental Psychology, 40A*, 239–268.

Goswami, U. (1989). Relational complexity and the development of analogical reasoning. *Cognitive Development, 4*, 251–268.

Goswami, U. (1990) A special link between rhyming skill and the use of orthographic analogies by beginning readers? *Journal of Child Psychology and Psychiatry, 31*, 301–311.

Goswami, U. (1991a). Analogical reasoning: What develops? A review of research and theory. *Child Development, 62*, 1–22.

Goswami, U. (1991b). Learning about spelling sequences in reading: The role of onsets and rimes. *Child Development, 62*, 1110–1123.

Goswami, U. & Brown, A.L. (1989). Melting chocolate and melting snowmen: Analogical reasoning and causal relations. *Cognition, 35*, 69–95.

Goswami, U. & Brown, A.L. (1990). Higher-order structure and relational reasoning: Contrasting analogical and thematic relations. *Cognition, 36*, 207–226.

Goswami, U. & Bryant, P.E. (1990). *Phonological skills and learning to read.* Hove: Lawrence Erlbaum Associates Ltd.

Goswami, U. & Mead, F. (1992). Onset and rime awareness and analogies in reading. *Reading Research Quarterly, 27*, 152–162.

Grudin, J. (1980). Processes in verbal analogy solution. *Journal of Experimental Psychology: Human Perception and Performance, 6*, 67–74.

Halford, G.S. (in press). *Children's understanding: The development of mental models.* Hillsdale, N.J.: Lawrence Erlbaum Associates Inc.

Harris, P.L. (1983). Infant cognition. In P. Mussen (Ed.), *Handbook of child psychology*, Vol. 2, pp. 758–769. New York: John Wiley.

Hart, K.M. (1980). *Secondary school children's understanding of mathematics.* Research Monograph. Chelsea College, University of London.

Haskell, R.E. (1989). Analogical transforms: A cognitive theory of the origin and development of equivalence transformations. *Metaphor and Symbolic Activity, 4*, 247–277.

Hayes, D.A. & Tierney, R.J. (1982). Developing readers' knowledge through analogy. *Reading Research Quarterly, 17*, 256–280.

Holyoak, K.J. & Koh, K. (1987). Surface and structural similarity in analogical transfer. *Memory and Cognition, 15*, 332–340.

Holyoak, K.J., Junn, E.N., & Billman, D.O. (1984). Development of analogical problem-solving skill. *Child Development, 55*, 2042–2055.

Hughes, M. (1986). *Children and number: Difficulties in learning mathematics.* Oxford: Basil Blackwell.

Inagaki, K. & Hatano, G. (1991). Constrained person analogy in young children's biological inference. *Cognitive Development, 6*, 219–231.

Inhelder, B. & Piaget, J. (1958). *The growth of logical thinking from childhood to adolescence.* New York: Basic Books.

Lamsfuss, S. & Wilkening, F. (1991). *False analogies in children's reasoning about interaction of forces.* Poster presented at the Biennial Meeting of the Society for Research in Child Development, Seattle, WA., April.

Levinson, P.J. & Carpenter, R.L. (1974). An analysis of analogical reasoning in children. *Child Development, 45*, 857–861.

Lunzer, E.A. (1965). Problems of formal reasoning in test situations. In P.H. Mussen (Ed.), *European research in child development.* Monographs of the Society for Research in Child Development, Vol. 30 (2, Serial number 100), pp. 19–46.

Mandler, J. (1992). How to build a baby II: Conceptual primitives. *Psychological Review, 99*.

Markman, E. & Hutchinson, J. (1984). Children's sensitivity to constraints on word meaning: Taxonomic versus thematic relations. *Cognitive Psychology, 16*, 1–27.

Marks, L.E., Hammeal, R.J., & Bornstein, M.H. (1987). *Perceiving similarity and comprehending metaphor.* Monographs of the Society for Research in Child Development, Vol. 52 (1, Serial number 215).

Marsh G., Friedman M.P., Welch V., & Desberg P. (1980). A cognitive-developmental approach to reading acquisition. In G.E. MacKinnon & T.G. Waller (Eds.), *Reading research: Advances in theory and practice*, Vol. 3, pp. 199–221. New York: Academic Press.

Massey, C.M. & Gelman, R. (1988). Preschooler's ability to decide whether a photographed unfamiliar object can move itself. *Developmental Psychology, 24*, 307–317.

Meltzoff, A.N. (1990). Foundations for developing a concept of self: Role of imitation in relating self to other and the value of social mirroring, social modelling and self-practice in infancy. In D. Cicchetti & M. Beeghly (Eds.), *The self in transition: Infancy to childhood*, pp. 139–164. Chicago: University of Chicago Press.

Meltzoff, A.N. & Moore, M.K. (1977). Imitation of facial and manual gestures by human neonates. *Science, 198*, 75–78.

Meltzoff, A.N. & Moore, M.K. (1983). Newborn infants imitate adult facial gestures. *Child Development, 54*, 702–709.

Nelson, K. (1977). The syntagmatic–paradigmatic shift revisited: A review of research and theory. *Psychological Bulletin, 84*, 93–116.

Nippold, M.A. & Sullivan, M.P. (1987). Verbal and perceptual analogical reasoning and proportional metaphor comprehension in young children. *Journal of Speech and Hearing Research, 30*, 367–376.

Palincsar, A.S. & Brown, A.L. (1984). Reciprocal teaching of comprehension-fostering and monitoring activities. *Cognition and Instruction, 1*, 117–175.

Palmer, S.E. (1989). Levels of description in information-processing theories of analogy. In S. Vosniadou & A. Ortony (Eds.), *Similarity and analogical reasoning*, pp. 332–345. Cambridge: Cambridge University Press.

Piaget, J., Montangero, J., & Billeter, J. (1977). Les correlats. In J. Piaget (Ed.), *L'Abstraction Reflechissante*. Paris: Presses Universitaires de France.

Ratterman, M.J., Gentner, D., & Deloache, J.S. (1987). *Young children's use of relational similarity in a transfer task.* Paper presented at the Biennial Meeting of the Society for Research in Child Development, Baltimore, MD, April.

Ratterman, M.J., Gentner, D., & Deloache, J.S. (in prep.). *The effect of language on similarity: Evidence from children's performance in an analogical mapping task.* Department of Psychology, University of Illinois at Urbana-Champaign, Ill.

Resnick, L.B. & Omanson, S.F. (1987). Learning to understand arithmetic. In R. Glaser (Ed.), *Advances in instructional psychology*, Vol. 3, pp. 41–95. Hillsdale, N.J.: Lawrence Erlbaum Associates Inc.

Schultz, T. R. (1982). *Rules of causal attribution.* Monographs of the Society for Research in Child Development, Vol. 47 (1, Serial number 194).

Siegal, M. (1991). *Knowing children: Experiments in conversation and cognition.* Hove: Lawrence Erlbaum Associates Ltd.

Siegal, M. & Smith, J.A. (1990). *Fractions, artifacts and natural kinds.* Paper presented at the International Congress of Applied Psychology, Kyoto, Japan, July.

Simons, P.R.J. (1984). Instructing with analogies. *Journal of Educational Psychology, 76,* 513–527.

Smiley, S.S. & Brown, A.L. (1979). Conceptual preference for thematic or taxonomic relations: A nonmonotonic age trend from preschool to old age. *Journal of Experimental Child Psychology, 28,* 249–257.

Spinillo, A.G. & Bryant, P.E. (1991). Children's proportional judgements: The importance of "half". *Child Development, 62,* 427–440.

Spiro, R.J., Feltovich, P.J., Coulson, R.L., & Anderson, D.K. (1989). Multiple analogies for complex concepts: Antidotes for analogy-induced misconception in advanced knowledge acquisition. In S. Vosniadou & A. Ortony (Eds.), *Similarity and analogical reasoning*, pp. 498–531. Cambridge: Cambridge University Press.

Stallard, A. (1982). *Children's understanding of written arithmetical symbolism.* Unpublished M.A. thesis, University of Edinburgh.

Sternberg, R.J. (1977). Component processes in analogical reasoning. *Pyschological Review, 84,* 353–378.

Sternberg, R.J. & Nigro, G. (1980). Developmental patterns in the solution of verbal analogies. *Child Development, 51,* 27–38.

Sternberg, R.J. & Rifkin, B. (1979). The development of analogical reasoning processes. *Journal of Experimental Child Psychology, 27,* 195–232.

Stuart, J.E. (1977). *Picture Test A.* Windsor: NFER-Nelson.

Treiman, R. (1988). The internal structure of the syllable. In G. Carlson & M. Tanenhaus (Eds.), *Linguistic structure in language processing*. Dordrecht: Kluver.

Vosniadou, S. (1989). Analogical reasoning as a mechanism in knowledge acquisition: A developmental perspective. In S. Vosniadou & A. Ortony (Eds.), *Similarity and analogical reasoning*, pp. 413–437. Cambridge: Cambridge University Press.

Vosniadou, S. & Ortony, A. (1983). The influence of analogy in children's acquisition of new information from text: An exploratory study. In J.A. Niles & L.A. Harris (Eds.), *Searches for meaning in reading/language processing and instruction*, pp. 71–79. Rochester, N.Y.: National Reading Conference.

Vosniadou, S. & Ortony, A. (1989). *Similarity and Analogical Reasoning*. Cambridge: Cambridge University Press.

Wagner, S., Winner, E., Cicchetti, D., & Gardner, H. (1981). "Metaphorical" mapping in human infants. *Child Development, 52*, 728–731.

White, T.G. & Cunningham, P.M. (1990). *Teaching disadvantaged students to decode by analogy*. Paper presented at the annual meeting of the American Educational Research Association, Boston, Mass. April.

Willner, A. (1964). An experimental analysis of analogical reasoning. *Psychological Reports, 15*, 479–494.

# Author Index

# Subject Index

# PHONOLOGICAL SKILLS AND LEARNING TO READ

## USHA GOSWAMI, (Cambridge University)
## PETER BRYANT, (Oxford University)

*"Goswami and Bryant assemble an impressive number of research studies which bear on their thesis, outlining them clearly and succinctly. They write persuasively but never dogmatically, revealing a refreshing willingness to give credit to theoretical positions other than their own. This book deserves serious attention by all those who are keen to relate the practice of the teaching of reading to theory which is firmly grounded in careful empirical work."* **Katherine Perera,** (The Times Higher Education Supplement).

*"I think this is an excellent and timely book. It has been a pleasure reviewing it."* **Dr Charles Hulme** (Reader in Psychology, University of York)

This book sets out to integrate recent exciting research on the precursors of reading and early reading strategies adopted by children in the classroom. It aims to develop a theory about why early phonological skills are crucial in learning to read, and shows how phonological knowledge about rhymes and other units of sound helps children learn about letter sequences when beginning to be taught to read.

The authors begin by contrasting theories which suggest that children's phonological awareness is a result of the experience of learning to read and those that suggest that phonological awareness precedes, and is a causal determinant of, reading. The authors argue for a version of the second kind of theory and show that children are aware of speech units, called onset and rime, before they learn to read and spell. An important part of the argument is that children make analogies and inferences about these letter sequences in order to read and write new words.

*Contents*: Preface. Phonological Awareness and Reading. How Children Read Words. Spelling and Phonological Awareness. How Children Read and Write New Words. Comparisons with Backward Readers and Spellers.Correlations and Longitudinal Predictions. Teaching Children About Sounds. Do Children Read (And Fail to Learn to Read) in Different Ways From Each Other? Theories About Learning to Read.

*Please send USA & Canadian orders to: Lawrence Erlbaum Associates Inc., 365 Broadway, Hillsdale, New Jersey, NJ07642, USA. For UK & Rest of World, please send orders to: Lawrence Erlbaum Associates Ltd., Mail Order Department, 27 Church Road, Hove, East Sussex, BN3 2FA, England. Note, prices shown here are correct at time of going to press, but may change. Prices outside Europe may differ from those shown.*

*Other Titles in the Series*
## Essays in Developmental Psychology
*Series Editors: Peter Bryant, George Butterworth, Harry McGurk*

# LANGUAGE EXPERIENCE AND EARLY LANGUAGE DEVELOPMENT
*From Input to Uptake*
## MARGARET HARRIS (University of London)

*"This is an extremely important contribution to the Essays in Developmental Psychology series. Written in a style which is lucid and readily accessible to the non-specialist, Harris presents an engaging account of the processes of language development during infancy and early childhood...it will be read with profit by undergraduate and postgraduate students concerned to understand the role of early experience in language development and how it interacts with biological endowment. Research students in particular will find the sections on methodology extremely helpful."* **H. McGurk** (Thomas Coram Research Unit, London).

This book is about one of the most fundamental debates on language development, namely the relationship between children's language development and their language experience. This issue is not only of theoretical interest: understanding how a child's language development is related to experience, has important implications for children whose early language development is giving cause for concern. If there are no environmental influences on early development then little can be done to help the child whose first steps into language are faltering. But, if the speed with which children develop language is subject to some external influence, then there are likely to be opportunities for successful intervention and grounds for optimism rather than pessimism in this area. This book argues that there are grounds for optimism.

*Contents:* Language and the Environment: Some Evidence from Chomsky, Children and Chimpanzees. Language Development and Adult Speech. The Social Context of Early Language Experience. From Input to Uptake: Traversing a Methodological Minefield. What Adults Say to Children. Language Experience and Vocabulary Development. The Establishment and Development of Word Meaning. Early Language Development in Deaf Children. Language. Language Experience and Early Language Development.

*0-86377-231-5 176pp. $35.95 £19.95 hb/0-86377-238-2 176pp. $16.50 £8.95 pb*

*Please send USA & Canadian orders to: Lawrence Erlbaum Associates Inc., 365 Broadway, Hillsdale, New Jersey, NJ07642, USA. For UK & Rest of World, please send orders to: Lawrence Erlbaum Associates Ltd., Mail Order Department, 27 Church Road, Hove, East Sussex, BN3 2FA, England. Note, prices shown here are correct at time of going to press, but may change. Prices outside Europe may differ from those shown.*